ELAYNA CARAUSU has been sailing the world for the past eleven years, traveling over 90,000 nautical miles. She's now a mother of two beautiful boys, which sparked the inspiration for this book.

The Little Sailor's ABCs is her first published book and was written at sea where her imagination runs wild. She's humbled to be able to share little pieces of the experience through this journey from A to Z. She has since published a second children's book titled *First Mate Lenny*, which tells the story of her firstborn, Lenny, on his exciting adventure as he learns the ropes onboard.

You can see more of the real life, magical visuals from their voyage in video at Youtube.com/sailinglavagabonde

I0224344

Also by Elayna Carausu

The Little Sailor's ABCs

First Mate Lenny

VAGABONDE
Kids

Elayna Carausu

SilverWood

Published in 2025 by SilverWood Books

SilverWood Books Ltd
14 Small Street, Bristol, BS1 1DE, United Kingdom
www.silverwoodbooks.co.uk

Text copyright © Elayna Carausu 2025
Images by kind permission of the sailing families
Cover image © Jorge Brillembourg & Steve Boxall

This book is here to share ideas, experiences, and inspiration about an
alternative lifestyle. It's not a manual or a set of rules, and it certainly
isn't professional, legal, or medical advice. Everyone's circumstances are
different, and what works well for one person may not be right for another.
Please use your own judgment, do your own research, and seek expert
guidance when needed before making big changes or decisions.
Neither the author nor the publisher can take responsibility for how the
information is used, but we hope it sparks curiosity and helps you explore
new possibilities in a safe and thoughtful way.

ISBN 978-1-80042-315-2 (paperback)
Also available as an ebook

Page design and typesetting by SilverWood Books

To all the parents raising little wanderers, chasing sunsets and making the world their classroom.

Contents

Chapter 1   *Introduction*   9

Part I

Chapter 2   *New crew*   31

Chapter 3   *Babies and toddlers*   50

Chapter 4   *The pre-school years*   74

Chapter 5   *Primary to pre-teens*   94

Chapter 6   *Sailing with teens*   125

Part II

Chapter 7   *Your floating home*   148

Chapter 8   *Work to cruise, cruise to work*   162

Chapter 9   *Health and safety*   180

Chapter 10   *Do it your way*   202

Resources   213

Acknowledgements   217

Chapter 1

Introduction

In 2018, Riley and I were sitting in a hospital in Antigua, nervously awaiting x-ray results and feeling anxious about what the future might hold. We had just crossed the Atlantic aboard our Outremer catamaran, *La Vagabonde II*, from the Spanish Canary Islands to Antigua. It wasn't our first Atlantic crossing, so we were filled with excitement and confidence as we cast off the lines for what we expected to be a fifteen-day crossing. We couldn't have predicted the trauma that was about to unfold. Five days into the passage, Riley had a freak accident. As he went to sit on the navigation chair, a wave bounced the boat, throwing him across the saloon and causing him to hit the top of his head on the saloon table. He briefly lost all feeling in his left arm and had severe pain in his neck for the rest of the voyage. We were both convinced he'd broken his neck.

Let me give you some back story. Back in 2010, before I met him, he'd broken his neck in a body surfing accident in Rio de Janeiro. Emergency surgery to insert a titanium and bone plate on his C6 and C7 vertebrae had damaged his vocal cord and left him unable to speak for six months. Now, we were terrified, just the two of us in the middle of the Atlantic Ocean, that the screw that held his vertebrae together was loose or broken. The next ten days were grim; Riley sailing with a potential life changing or even fatal injury and both of us fearing the prognosis that awaited when or if he made land. Our precarious situation, out there on the vast ocean, reminded us of how precious and fragile life is. Upon making land in Antigua, Riley went for an x-ray. When the result revealed that the bang to his head had caused no further neck damage, we were flooded with relief. We quite literally looked at each other and said, "Let's have a baby!"

That was it. The moment that changed everything aboard *La Vagabonde II*, when we decided to leave behind childless, carefree, minimal planning cruising. When we said goodbye to pulling all-nighters to get to where we wanted to go or to complete work projects. When we turned our backs on spontaneous decisions about our next destination or what we'd do when we dropped anchor. When our choices about sailing in crazy weather and rough sea conditions were no longer based on our own safety. We swapped all that for a more challenging, but infinitely more rewarding, cruising life with kids.

Little did we know how quickly and dramatically a tiny new crew member would turn our cruising life upside down. People assumed that sailing with a baby would be too challenging and we'd soon opt for a more settled (read: 'landlubber') life. However, either through naïve optimism or sheer determination, we discovered that with some careful planning and forethought, our amazing sailing adventure could continue, now as a family, and that we would discover the world anew, this time through the eyes of our children.

Riley and I met in Greece in 2014, shortly after he'd bought the original *La Vagabonde*. Neither of us had much sailing experience, but we had a passion to learn and to explore the world by boat. Since those early days, we've been passionate about sharing our love of sailing and encouraging others to follow their sailing dreams too. With the birth of Lenny in 2018 and Darwin in 2021, that passion has evolved and we now want to share what we've learned about family cruising and encourage other families to take the plunge, whether for a family boating holiday, a short- or longer-term sabbatical from work and school, or an all-in, open-ended commitment to cruising life.

Like most new parents, we were pretty clueless about how to care for our new baby. Sure, there are lots of parenting books, blogs, websites, and advice out there. But not too many about how to parent aboard a yacht. We scraped together what advice we could from blogging and vlogging cruising parents, from Facebook groups and websites, and from books written by cruising moms. (You'll find links to resources scattered throughout the info boxes and at the end of the book). We observed what other cruising families around us were doing and took advice from more experienced parents. Through trial and error, we figured out what worked for our specific lifestyle, on our specific boat, and for our personalities. Over the years, we've learned a lot about being a 'floating family'. We've discovered what works and what doesn't and we're still on our parenting journey. As I write, Lenny has begun home schooling and Darwin isn't far behind, and that's opened up a whole new chapter in our cruising lives. We continue to look to other cruising families for inspiration, squirreling away nuggets of advice that give us the confidence to face each new childhood milestone and each new challenge as the boys grow and our family life evolves.

So many questions

Riley and I love sharing our experiences and encouraging other dreamers to become sailors too. That's one of the main reasons why I wanted to write this book. It is also inspired by the questions I get asked almost daily via our *Sailing La Vagabonde* channel and my Instagram account, at boat shows and other public appearances, and from people we meet when we're out and about. Some questions come from people who are simply curious about how we raise our children on a boat. Others come from parents who are actively planning to make the transition to a cruising lifestyle, or from childless cruisers who are thinking about becoming parents.

People want to know about the nuts and bolts of day-to-day cruising with children, and their questions broadly fall into a few categories:

- Safety and danger: Kid-proofing the boat. Keeping the boys safe when we're sailing. Protecting them from the sun. Dealing with illness or medical emergencies.

- Play: Keeping the boys occupied. Keeping toys to a minimum. Boat-friendly toys and activities.

- Education: Current education practices and future plans. Concerns about the boys falling behind their school-going peers.

- Socialization: Making friends. Maintaining relationships with grandparents and other family members.

- Childhood development: Learning to walk/ride bicycles/swim while living on a boat.

- Food: Provisioning the boat with children in mind. Dealing with allergies or with fussy eaters, especially when we sail to different countries and regions of the world.

- Sleep: Best sleeping arrangements with kids on board. Our bedtime routine.

- Kid paraphernalia: Nappies, car seats, strollers, high chairs. Making excursions off the boat.

- Work and family life: Raising kids while working and sailing full time. Our schedules/routines. Living together 24/7 in such a small space. Making space for each other.

Living this life all day every day, it's easy to forget that much of what we do seems difficult or strange to people who have never been on a boat. Martina Tyrrell, one of the contributors to this book (I'll get to those very soon), said she was surprised by the questions she was asked when her family was making the transition to boat life. "I thought our parents would have lots of questions about danger – heavy weather and pirates and sailing in unsafe waters. In fact, what they wanted to know was how we would do laundry, where the children would sleep, and if we'd have a fridge on board." Indeed, for many people, the minutiae of daily life on a boat with children can seem daunting. That's why I've decided to write a book that will give parents the confidence to sail with their children, for no matter how long and no matter the age of their children.

Vagabond families

Like all families, mine is unique, and filling a book with our experiences alone would be quite limited. Sailing families come in all shapes and sizes, with children of different ages, living on big boats and small boats, on big budgets and small budgets. Some families have plans to return to jobs and homes on land after a year or two of cruising, while others have untied their mooring lines and sailed into the wild blue yonder indefinitely. Few families have enough resources to not have to worry about work, so most continue to work in one manner or another to finance their lifestyles. Sailing families come from all over the world and cruise in all the world's oceans. Some parents, such as Riley and myself, were already cruising before children came along. Others decided to embark on this lifestyle when their children were babies, toddlers, pre-teens, or teens. In other words, every cruising family has a unique experience, and there are families out there who know a lot more about certain aspects of family cruising, such as, for example, moving aboard as a family, the challenges of making and maintaining friendships for older children, and cruising with teens as they prepare for adulthood.

So, I invited other cruising families to share their experiences and insights. In addition to the practicalities of cruising, I wanted to know about the challenges and joys of living on a boat with children, and about how cruising practice and family relationships have evolved over time. Cheeky confession: I've also gathered all of these fantastic insights to help my family through the years ahead.

Asking cruising parents to share their thoughts and advice is all well and good. Setting sail is likely to have been their idea in the first place. They're probably going to tell me how rosy and perfect it all is. But what about the kids? What are their thoughts about this crazy adventure their parents are taking them on. Do they love it? Do they miss a more conventional life and more conventional friendships? Do they think that homeschooling is the greatest idea ever or do they wish for a teacher other than their mum, dad, and YouTube? I decided to ask some older sailing kids about the highs and lows of living in a floating home. Their answers were both delightful and surprising.

The result is a collaboration with seven amazing cruising families who took the time to share their skills, experience, and advice and who are just as passionate about sailing with their kids as we are.

Kim and **Bart Kroon** and 3-year-old[1] **Liz** are from the Netherlands and live aboard *Tranquillity*, a Scanmar 33. Bart is a nurse anesthetist and Kim was a products manager at a bank. They bought *Tranquillity* in 2008 and, while Bart would have taken the leap to sell their house and set sail immediately, Kim admits to having been more career-minded and imagining a six-month sabbatical from her

---

1   All ages are the ages of the children at the time of interview, in early 2022.

job "in a few years' time." However, three weeks before Liz was born, Kim's mother died suddenly. In the chaotic months that followed, as Kim coped with the grief of losing her mother while caring for her new baby, she thought about her mother's approach to life. "Always chase your dream," her mother used to say. "If you have a dream, don't postpone it." When the COVID-19 pandemic hit, and Bart and Kim's travel plans were scrapped, they decided to go on a family holiday on their boat instead. "One night, I was in the cockpit and all of a sudden it was clear to me – if I postpone everything, it might never happen," Kim recalls. "So, I asked Bart, 'What do we have to do if we want to leave next year?'" Most recently, the family were on the island of Curaçao in the Caribbean.

Jessica and Jeroen Scherpenzeel and Benjamin (5) and Frank (4), are also from the Netherlands, and live aboard *Sans Souci*, a Harmony 47. One day, some years ago, Jeroen was sailing alone in a boat given to him by his grandfather. He passed a little open boat with four girls on board. 'Why am I sailing alone,' he thought to himself. When he went home, he Googled 'sailing girls' and 'sailing women' (we're not judging you, Jeroen, honest!). Guess what he found? My YouTube video 'Why every sailor needs a girl on board' (check it out...you'll see why feminine energy is the antidote to isolation at sea!) and that was the gateway drug to our *Sailing La Vagabonde* channel. "We started dreaming that one day we'd do it too," Jessica says. "And then, one day, we thought, 'What if one day doesn't come?' We know people who got sick or died at a young age, so we didn't want to wait." They bought *Sans Souci* in 2020 and moved aboard. Most recently, they were in Martinique in the Caribbean.

Juliana Licht and Valentin Hadelich and Arvin (15), Levin (12), Jason (9), and Taron (6) are German and live aboard *Argo*, a 52-foot Beaufort 16. When their usual family holiday destination was booked out, a friend suggested they holiday in Maasholm, near

Germany's border with Denmark, on the Baltic Sea. One day, as they were walking along the harbor, the four boys spotted a tall ship. "Before we could do anything, they were on board, talking to the captain," Valentin said. "He ended up inviting us to sail with him the next day. That was the first ever sailing experience for all six of us." At the time, Valentin, an architect, lived in Hamburg during the week and his job took him around Europe, while Juliana, who works with blind children, lived with the boys at their family home in Wismar. "It was fine," Valentin recalls, "but also, I was missing a lot." That serendipitous day sail in Maasholm changed everything. "I started to watch YouTube channels," Valentin says, including *Sailing La Vagabonde* and that of a German family. A spark had been ignited and there was no turning back. They bought *Argo* in Greece and learned to sail her on the voyage from the east Mediterranean to their home port of Lubeck on the Baltic Sea. They are currently living aboard on a one-and-a-half-year sabbatical and were most recently back in Greece again.

Sara and **Lee Rice** and **Taj** (17) and **Bella** (16) are from Australia's Gold Coast and live aboard *Catalpa II*, a Pearson 530. Sara was a yoga instructor and Lee was in the building and then the mining industries. A year before they set sail, the couple started their own yoga business. Although life was good, they felt that something was missing. "Work and school commitments just weren't us. We weren't living our true selves," Sara says. The death of her mother when Sara was 21 and becoming a new mum herself instilled a sense of the shortness of life. "Mum and Dad were waiting until they retired to go off and live the dream." When Lee's dad died a few years later, they thought "What are we doing? You get these little moments when you realize that you want to enjoy the time you have with your kids and not wait until they've moved out and left home. We wanted to do it with them, to share the experiences, the traveling, the learning, everything with them." They bought ferro-cement *Catalpa* to sail to the Whitsunday Islands on a family holiday. "Financially, it seemed smarter to spend the money on a boat than on a single holiday." They replaced her with *Catalpa II* in 2022 and most recently were on the Pacific coast of Mexico.

Allan 'Woody' Wood and **Irenka Griffin**, and **Rowan** (16), **Darry** (13), and **Yewan** (11) are an English family who live aboard their 52-foot Amel Super Maramu, *Mothership*. Woody and Irenka met in Greece, where they were both flotilla skippers and returned to the UK to set up their own sailing school. Before that, Irenka was a drama and movement therapist in prisons and hospitals, and with people with disabilities, and Woody was a computer games artist. Irenka dreamed of sailing around the world since she was 10 years old. They bought *Mothership* in Greece in 2017 and began their circumnavigation. Most recently, Woody, Irenka, and the two boys were in Rangitoto Island, northern New Zealand, and Rowan was in southwest London, completing her education.

Martina Tyrrell and **Julian Scott** and **Lily** and **Katie** are an Irish and British family. They lived aboard Westerly Conway *Carina of Devon* for six years, first moving aboard when the girls were 3 and 1 years old. "My dad and Julian's step-dad both died from cancer at a young age. That brought home to us the shortness and unpredictability of life." Martina was an anthropologist who worked in the Arctic and Julian was an Antarctic geophysicist, before they quit their jobs and bought their boat, fulling a dream they'd had since they first met. For six years, they mixed cruising Europe's western seaboard with longer periods at anchor in the UK and Spain. In 2016, they enrolled Lily and Katie in a rural Spanish school as a way to immerse them in Spanish language and culture. Two years later, the family decided to make Spain their home. They sold *Carina* in 2019. Julian died suddenly in 2021. "Looking back, I'm really glad we took the plunge into live aboard life when we did," Martina says.

Carola and Teddy[2] and **Ellen** and **Timmy** are a Dutch and German family. Both Carola and Teddy were inland waterways captains in the Netherlands before they met. Teddy already owned *Maes*, a 65-foot 1930s German Baltic patrol vessel. Carola gave birth to both Ellen (now 21) and Timmy (now 17) aboard *Maes*. The children attended school in Amsterdam from their home aboard the boat, and spent summers and holidays cruising in Dutch and UK waters. Most recently, Carola and Teddy are aboard *Maes* on the Spanish-Portuguese border, Timmy lives in the Netherlands aboard a barge inherited from his grandparents, and Ellen has chosen a land-based life with her boyfriend, who also grew up on a boat.

Hazel and **Dave McCabe** and **Katie** and **Reuben** are a British family who lived aboard *Ros Ailither*, a 50-foot wooden Killybegs trawler, for 14 years. Hazel, a wood carver, and Dave, a boat builder, lived aboard and ran a ferry on the south coast of England before buying *Ros Ailither*. Katie (now 17) was taken home to *Ros Ailither* when only a few weeks old and Reuben (now 13) was born onboard. The family lived aboard in southern England, and took a number of long-term sabbaticals from formal education to cruise in western and southern Europe and to cross the Atlantic. In 2019, the family decided to sell *Ros Ailither* and move ashore. They continue to own sailing boats and to sail recreationally. In 2021, then 14-year-old Katie became the youngest person to solo sail around Great Britain, doing so in *Falanda*, a 26-foot wooden sloop that she bought and restored by herself when she was 13.

And, finally, there's me, **Elayna Carausu**, my partner **Riley Whitlum** and **Lenny** (5) and **Darwin** (3). We're Australian and live aboard *La Vagabonde III*. I was a singer and dive instructor when I met Riley

---

2   Carola and Teddy have asked that their surname not be included.

in Greece in 2014. At the time, he was living aboard his 43-foot Beneteau Cyclades, *La Vagabonde*, and financing his sailing lifestyle with regular trips back to Western Australia to work offshore in the oil and gas industry. Over the past ten years, we've sailed more than 50,000 nautical miles, created a successful YouTube channel, *Sailing La Vagabonde*, moved from the original monohull *La Vagabonde* to *La Vagabonde II*, a 48-foot Outremer catamaran that we moved aboard in 2017, to *La Vagabonde III*, a 60-foot bespoke trimaran that we've been living aboard since the start of 2024. (If they invent a four-hull yacht, it looks like we're going there next!). Lenny and Darwin have been cruising kids since they were babies.

What a range of experience! From newly fledged sailors to parents who have been sailing most of their lives; from small modern GPR yachts to adapted fishing vessels; from families who have just started their journey to families who have changed direction to pursue different paths. Each family has its own unique story and its own unique way of raising children. Yet, beneath those differences they share common approaches to life and to parenting, and to safety, education, and health and wellbeing. The spark or the push for some families was the untimely death of loved ones and the realization that life is short; the spark for all was a desire to spend more time together as a family and to be more active in their children's lives. The common theme among all the families is the idea of living a hybrid cruising life. And that was the third key inspiration for writing this book at this moment in time.

Hybrid cruising – the best of all worlds

Those inspirational families give me comfort and hope. As a cruising parent (let's face it, as any parent), you are constantly made to feel that you're doing it wrong. First, there are the books, blogs, and social media accounts that give the impression that cruising is an all-or-nothing pursuit. You untie your mooring lines from your home port and that's it. You're on your own, your own little kingdom. You eat from your spear. You make money from your canvas sewing/engine repair/landscape painting/vlogging (ahem, I'm looking at you in the mirror) skills. You invent your own homeschooling method for your kids, even though you have no teaching experience. You make and mend and repair everything on board. You entertain yourselves with your kids amazing musical talents. Your life is your boat and the sea. That's it.

But the families I have met over the past few years and the families who've contributed their wisdom to this book are much more fluid and nuanced in their approaches to cruising. They travel at sea when it suits them, and remain in place (on their boat or on land) for periods of time to work or to expose their kids to formal education and different cultures. This is a much more blended and manageable approach to living aboard.

It took me a long time to realize that cruising doesn't have to be all or nothing. For instance, I had it in my head that because we are a live aboard family, we had to homeschool Lenny and Darwin on our own, entirely without help. That scared the hell out of me. But when I thought about taking a more hybrid approach to education, I felt like a fraud because putting the kids in kindergarten or in school now and again wasn't hard core enough. I want to save you the time it took me to come to this realization by sharing a range of different approaches to cruising life, to show you there's no right or wrong way to do it. The only way to do it is the way that suits your family.

Pretty much every cruising family out there takes a hybrid approach. They pick and choose the parts of cruising life that suit their family's educational needs, financial needs, and personalities. And what suits them evolves over time as their families grow (physically and/or in head count).

Taking the leap to a life at sea can be scary, especially if you (and those around you) imagine that it has to be all or nothing. For one reason or another, most families can't simply untie their lines and sail off into the sunset without a backward glance. Most of us have to earn money, and many have ongoing work or family commitments that keep us closer to home.

I wanted to write a cruising book that incorporates all the changes that have happened in the past few years. Information technology and digital technology make cruising with kids easier than ever. Nomadic and distance work, education, shopping, and socializing can now be done pretty much everywhere (to quote Taj on *Catalpa II*, "Starlink's a game changer"). The COVID-19 pandemic helped us all to develop innovative ways to work, learn, and stay in touch with loved ones. Some sailing families had been doing that stuff for years, but the pandemic put in place practices and social norms that allow a lot more people to do it now. The pandemic also helped people to see what is important in their lives. For many, that included spending more time with their children and learning and growing alongside them.

This book, therefore, contains tips and advice for living a successful hybrid cruising life told through our own experiences. The seven families and I share our approaches to education, socializing, safety, health and wellbeing, and work, while living in the small spaces of our floating homes and exploring the world on our terms and according to our timetables.

Crusty sea dog alert

You will meet a lot of amazing people when you go cruising with your children. Kind people. Funny people. People who have done things in their lives that will leave your jaw on the floor. One of the great joys of cruising is all the other amazing sailors you'll meet. But I'm going to let you in on a little secret. You're also going to meet a lot of sailors who are going to tell you you're not doing it right.

There will be crusty old Jack[3] who refuses to sully the pure art of sailing by having an electronic navigation system (or soap) on board. He'll tell you that you're not hard core enough because you're using electronic charts and you've hired a car to go exploring. There will be Jim and Trish, retired, with more money than sense, and with every mod-con imaginable on their shiny gin palace. They'll tell you that you can't possibly cruise with children without an American-style fridge freezer, a clothes dryer, a water maker, and every type of energy generator that's yet been invented. They'll also want to know why you're rushing around all the time and not relaxing and taking it easy. (Despite having kids of their own, they have no memory of this mad phase of life). And they'll want to know why you don't do something about all the shrieking and whooping and having fun that your children seem to be engaged in. There will be Blossom, the earth mother, who lives on a patched-up boat and whose kids run around naked all day long. She will look on you with disdain for using disposable nappies, for not making and mending your children's clothes, and for abusing them by letting them have ice cream when you go to the beach.

This book is an antidote for and a shield against all those know-it-alls, know-it-betters, busy bodies who will try to tell you how best to live your cruising life. For all the wonderful, caring, compassionate cruisers you'll meet (and there will be many), you will also encounter those who will tell you that, whatever you're doing, you're doing it wrong. They'll have opinions about how you educate your kids, what you feed your kids, your sleeping arrangements, what your kids play with, who they play with, how you hang your laundry out to dry. You name it, someone will have an opinion.

It can be pretty challenging to be constantly told that we're not doing it the *right* way, especially in parts of the world where

---

3   Names have been changed to protect the guilty.

cruising families aren't in abundance and you don't have other families to share your experience with. We're here to reassure you that, whether you want to live a blue water, off grid, cloth nappy, unschooled life, or you want to drop anchor for the school year, stick to coastal waters, continue in your corporate job, then you can find ways to make it work for your cruising family.

Right now, there are hundreds of families around the world, in oceans, at anchorages, and on docks, living the cruising life of their dreams. Right now, there's a kid doing homework at the saloon table in the middle of the Pacific and another playing on a beach with newfound yachtie friends in the Bahamas. Right now, there's a family snorkeling over a reef in Indonesia, hiking through a rainforest in Suriname, buying groceries at a market in Portugal. If that's your dream, then read on.

Let's dive in

Let me tell you what this book is *not* about. It's not about how to sail, or how to choose the right boat, or how to anchor in a tight spot, or how to heave to in heavy weather. Books on those topics could fill a library. Instead, it is all about how healthy and happy parents can raise healthy and happy children while living on a sailing vessel. It is for everyone from the seasoned sailors thinking about growing their own crew from seed to the landlubber parents wondering whether this is the life for their family.

The book is divided into two parts. Part I starts at pre-pregnancy and goes through the stages of childhood. I'll walk you through each stage of your child's liveaboard life and the different developmental, educational, socialization, health and safety, and other aspects of life that come to the fore at each stage. Part II explores work and finance, creating space in your home, health and safety, and preparing to move ashore. We don't have all the answers but, between us eight families, we have many years and tens of thousands of nautical miles of experience.

At the end of the book, there is a Resources section with links and descriptions to resources that we recommend. I hope these will help you dive even deeper into the topics that interest you.

We offer our experiences not to say 'this is how it should be done' but rather 'here's how we made it up as we went along. Maybe this will work for you; maybe it will inspire you to devise your own solution.' The most important thing is to have the courage to know that your way is the right way if it works for your family. Remember, sometimes it takes a little trial and error to figure out what works and what doesn't. Remember too that your cruising life with evolve over time as you gain more experience and as your children grow.

No matter how much or how little sailing experience you have, cruising with your family and transforming your boat into your temporary or permanent home will be a whole new experience. Your relationship with your boat will change; your relationship with your partner and your children will change. And, for me and for the lovely contributors to this book, it is our sincerest wish that those changes will be for the better. That your relationship with your boat and with the people you live with aboard will grow deeper and that you will have experiences and adventures together that will be beyond even your wildest dreams.

What are you waiting for? Let's go!

Part I

Kids on board

The boys and I paddled in the shallows in the turquoise waters off a Bahamian beach as the smell of smoked hogfish wafted over us. Riley was on the beach, indulging in his new passion for smoking fish. Earlier, two-and-a-half-year-old Lenny had marveled at the bright pink and red fish dad had spearfished and which Riley was now turning into a delicious and healthy source of protein that would last us for weeks stored in the fridge aboard La Vagabonde II. *The leaning coconut palms shaded us from the heat of the sun, and we spent hours in the water and on the beach, the boat gently swaying on anchor only 20 meters away. When he wasn't splashing in the water at the shoreline, six-month-old Darwin, who'd only recently mastered the skill of sitting up unsupported, sat in the soft white sand, moving small fistfuls of sand and shells around. He was clearly enjoying himself, but I kept a keen eye on him for the occasional fistfuls that started to make their way to his mouth. A baby reef shark came to the shoreline to scavenge some of the fish carcass that Riley threw away and Lenny squealed with delight. We sat in the sand and ate a late afternoon lunch of smoked fish, watching as the tropical humidity gave rise to an afternoon squall brewing on the horizon. I looked at the three of them – Riley and our two perfect boys – and I realized that we'd made it. This is what life is about – being in nature and learning the lessons she teaches us and, more than anything else, being at home with my family. I looked at our two little boys and realized we were just getting started.*

Welcome aboard. It's time to focus on the different stages in the lives of your littlest crew members. I'm often asked what is a good age to set sail with children. Are babies easier than toddlers? (In some ways, yes). Wouldn't older children prefer to be with their peers? (Some, maybe). Is home schooling teenagers beyond the abilities of most parents? (Definitely not...or so I'm told). There are challenges to cruising with children no matter what their age. But the rewards of exploring the world with your children, of watching them grow and develop, of growing together as a family, far outweigh all of those challenges.

Together with the rich and varied experiences of the contributing families, I'm here to put your mind at ease about cruising with your children. We've learned, through trial and error and from observing and talking to other families, what works and what doesn't, and we want to share that knowledge with you. The following chapters organically follow the life of a child onboard – from your pregnancy through to your little crew member spreading their wings and leaving home. For some children, such as Lenny and Darwin, the boat has always been home. Their experiences (and ours) are very different to those who move aboard as 3-year-olds, 8-year-olds, or 14-year-olds. I hope that recounting our varied experiences and sharing our advice will give you the confidence to raise your children on a boat in a way that is comfortable and sustainable for your family. There is no ideal age to take your kids cruising. At each developmental stage of your child's life, you will face different socialization, education, and health and safety challenges. But you

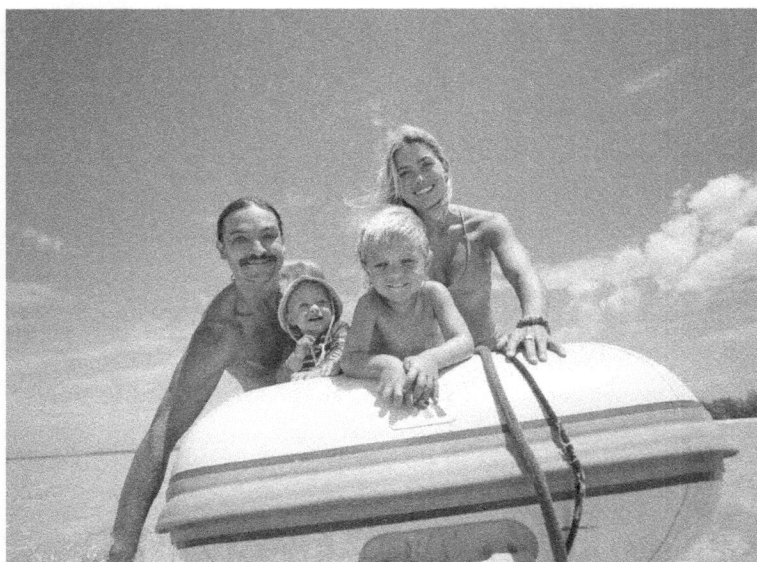

Riley, Darwin, Lenny and Elayna *(La Vagabonde II)*

know your own children better than anyone else, and together you'll find the way that works for you.

As you're about to discover, many of the challenges that cruising families face at different stages of their children's lives are similar; and while some deal with those in time-honored ways, others take more novel approaches. Our stories, tips and, sometimes, hard-earned wisdom, will give you the confidence to set sail with your children, no matter what their age. Your concerns and focus will differ depending on the age of your cruising child. While you might be more alert to water and boat safety issues with a baby or toddler, education and socialization may be a bigger focus with older children. And, as the younger members of your crew grow and develop, your focus will evolve. Not so different to kids on land, I guess.

Overcoming the challenge mindset

Let's not kid ourselves. Raising children anywhere is hard work. But I'm surprised at how often people ask me about the *challenges* of cruising with children, rather than the rich rewards. The challenge of keeping your baby safe, the challenge of getting from boat to shore with toddlers, the challenge of homeschooling, the challenge of finding other children for your kids to play with. Let's put this challenge mindset behind us and instead focus on the possibilities and rewards of cruising with our children.

Cruising parents will tell you that the richest reward of sailing with their children is being alongside them at every stage of their development, and seeing them blossom and grow. Jeroen says, "My father worked six days a week to make sure my mother didn't have to work. Even today, he hears stories about me and my siblings that he doesn't know about because he missed those moments when we were small. We don't have that. We get to see and be part of everything."

Sara believes that one of the biggest rewards of living aboard is doing and learning together as a family. She says, "There are so many rewards of this lifestyle. The time and experiences we have together. You see your kids have the biggest smiles on their faces because they're having such a good time, and then you have the same smile because you're having the best time too. It makes all the hard things worth it. I love that we made it work, this situation that so many people thought was impossible. It's made all four of us the people we are today."

Armed with knowledge for meeting negative feedback

So many people will support your decision to sail away with your kids. Family members, friends, and teachers will cheerlead you all the way. But not everyone. There will be some who won't be so supportive. "We got a lot of 'you're nuts. What's wrong with you?'" Sara admits. "A lot of people said we needed to buy a house, settle down, that the kids needed to be in school." But she and Lee had enough support to not be deterred by those negative comments. "My mother-in-law said, 'you're going to kill my grandchildren,'" Martina says. But she soon realized that a lot of the negativity from family and friends arose from lack of understanding. "I encouraged everyone to ask questions. I couldn't guarantee that I'd know the answers, but at least I'd know what their worries were. If I couldn't answer the question, it might be because it was an aspect of cruising life that I hadn't considered and I would need to investigate before setting sail." Martina's mum had a notepad where she wrote down her questions and worries. "Her questions were all very domestic. She'd never been on a boat before, so stepping on board *Carina* for the first time was a big revelation for her. It put a lot of her worries to rest."

This part of the book has all of those concerned family members and friends in mind. While this is, at its core, a guide for prospective sailing parents, it can also serve as a source of reassurance for worried loved ones, to prove that you're not the first parents to have this crazy dream, and that there is a huge worldwide community of cruising families out there with healthy, happy, educated, and well-adjusted kids.

Don't wait too long

The most important piece of advice that most cruisers will give is 'Don't wait too long.' Carola says, "Lots of people have a project. They want to build a boat; they want to sail. But then they get divorced or someone becomes ill, and they never achieve their dream. There's no good or bad time to sail. So long as you have a boat that's not going to sink, just do it."

Sara says, "If you can go now and feel comfortable about it, do it. Because if you don't do it now, then maybe you won't ever, and living with regret is far worse. As hard as it's been, it's been a beautiful, beautiful journey."

So, let's get started on this beautiful beautiful journey.

Chapter 2

New crew

That day in the hospital in Antigua, we made the impulsive decision to have a baby. A year earlier, we'd joked about having kids someday, but this time we were serious. Those scary days in the Atlantic made us think about how precious and precarious life is. We didn't want to wait any longer to share this beautiful life with another little soul. We were still in Antigua when I became pregnant, and things started to move pretty quickly, as we faced the start of a whole new life adventure.

If you're not already a cruiser, you might be surprised to know that a lot of couples continue to sail during pregnancy and some even choose to give birth aboard their floating homes. In this chapter, Hazel, Carola, and I share our experiences of cruising while pregnant, the challenges we faced, and our antenatal and birth decisions. And we share our birth stories because, let's face it, who doesn't love a good birth story? We each have two children and the experiences and learned we lessons from our first pregnancies prepared us for the second time around. Even if you don't ever plan to (or accidentally end up...yikes) pregnant while sailing, this chapter will show you that no matter what the situation, with some planning and forethought, you can make it work. And when things don't work out as planned, at whatever stage of your parenthood, the key to happiness and success is an open attitude and a willingness to go with the flow of changes over which you have little or no control.

Let's have a baby

For some long-term cruisers, such as Riley and me, starting a family feels like a natural progression of their live aboard life. Couples on shorter cruising sabbaticals are generally less likely to throw a pregnancy into the mix. Only a crazy person would throw having a baby into a sailing gap year or two, right? They're probably out there but, so far, I haven't tracked them down.

Just like me, Hazel on *Ros Ailither* and Carola on *Maes* became pregnant soon after they'd decided to start a family. In 2007, Hazel and Dave crossed the Atlantic, from the UK to the Caribbean. From there they sailed up the east coast of the US to Canada. "It was only a couple of months since we'd decided to try to have a baby. Neither of us imagined it would happen so quickly, and we were taken by surprise when I discovered I was pregnant in Canada!" Carola and Teddy had also just made the decision to have a baby when Carola found out she was pregnant. In fact, Carola is pretty sure that she became pregnant on the same day that she and Teddy decided to start trying! Speedy work! I chalk it up to all that fresh air and the active sailing lifestyle!

Healthy mama, healthy baby
Morning sickness

Like many mums-to-be, my initial joy at discovering I was pregnant was almost immediately tempered by anxiety for the health and welfare of my baby. Anxiety hovered over me for much of my first pregnancy, but I armed myself with knowledge and made sure I had lots of support both for me and my unborn baby.

Since I'd moved aboard *La Vagabonde* in 2014, I'd only been properly seasick twice and the prospect of morning sickness – or morning sickness morphing into seasickness, or vice versa – worried me. I'd heard anecdotes of women who'd never been troubled by seasickness – like the friend of a friend, a fisherman's daughter, who grew up on fishing boats on the east coast of Canada – who, as soon as she became pregnant, felt queasy every time they set foot on a boat. What if that happened to me? How could we continue sailing if I felt sick every day?[4]

While I worried about the practicalities of cruising with morning/seasickness, Hazel worried about harming her baby if she was sick a lot. She too had only rarely experienced seasickness, and then only under the worst sea conditions. To prepare for the worst, she sought advice from a doctor, who recommended drinking Gatorade to replenish sugar and salts. Luckily for Hazel, her worries were for nothing, as she experienced minimal morning sickness, and mostly carried on as normal.

Not so for me. Almost from the start of both pregnancies, I felt seasick on every passage, although I rarely vomited. At first, I spent most of the time when I wasn't on watch lying down in my cabin. I hated it. But I listened to my body as best I could and didn't push myself to be as active a crew member as usual.

By coincidence, around the time I found out I was pregnant with Lenny, we had our first 'official' crew member onboard. We'd often had friends and family members help out, but Stefan was the first person to come aboard with a specific crewing role. He took up a lot of the slack. Riley thought it was 'unfair' that I had do night watches, given my 'condition.' Who was I to argue with the skipper? Staying awake at night really messes up your system; so, we divided the watches between the three of us so that I always had the nights off. That took a lot of the pressure off me and my growing baby. I got plenty of rest at night and then was more mobile during the day.

---

4   In hindsight, I know this was an irrational fear. Seasickness, except in bad sailing conditions, tends to pass as your body gets used to the movements of the boat over time. As we'll see in the next chapter, mothers sometimes are more prone to seasickness because the demands of caring for small children are not conducive to keeping seasickness at bay.

A brief note on crew, which I'll return to in Chapter 10. Stefan was great and having an extra responsible adult really took the pressure off both Riley and me. But those two guys meant there was a lot of male energy on board at a time when I really craved female energy. My first pregnancy felt lonely at times and, in hindsight, I think I would have fared better with female crew. That feeling led to us, over time, hiring more female crew.

By the second trimester, I'd come out the other side of the queasiness. In hindsight, those physical feelings were compounded by negative emotions and I experienced dips in my mood that I couldn't explain at the time but which I realize now were related to feelings of anxiety about the health of the baby.

Zika virus

I had reason to feel anxious. From Antigua, we made our way to the US. Some of the islands along the way had experienced outbreaks of Zika virus in recent years. Some of our YouTube channel subscribers advised against going to those islands. To allay my anxiety, I set out to arm myself with knowledge. Finding up-to-date information online proved a challenge. Instead, I called the biggest hospital on each island prior to sailing there and asked for the phone number of the relevant department or institution responsible for disease control. It turned out that the virus had been most active two to three years earlier and no island had more than one or two confirmed cases per year.

The fact was, I was more likely to get hit on the head with a coconut than to contract Zika. Still, I took the precautions of wearing long linen clothing and keeping the saloon closed as much as possible to keep mosquitos out. My advice to any pregnant women traveling in parts of the world where Zika virus may exist is to get general advice from a reputable organization, such as the CDC or WHO, about how best to protect yourself and place-specific advice from regional or local institutions for disease control.

Zika virus

Zika virus has been reported in the United States, Central and South America, across central Africa and in south and southeast Asia. It is spread through the bite of an infected day-time active mosquito and (more rarely) by having unprotected sex with someone who has the virus, even if that person has no symptoms. Catching the virus during pregnancy can lead to serious birth defects, including serious brain and eye defects, problems with hearing, joint and movement limitations, and other problems. There is no vaccine to prevent Zika and no medicine to treat it. The US Centers for Disease Control and Preventions (CDC) provides useful up-to-date international travel information about Zika virus outbreaks, parts of the world where extra care should be taken, and precautions travelers should take. According to the World Health Organization, the virus has been in decline globally since 2017 (https://www.who.int/health-topics/zika-virus-disease).

Staying active

Living on a boat is about as active a lifestyle as you can get. Hoisting sails, hopping into and out of dinghies, lugging your groceries from the market back to the boat will all keep you in shape. Like most sailing mamas, I was already in good shape when I got pregnant. I didn't know if I could continue being as active as my bump grew bigger, but I found that with just a few adjustments, I was able to carry on pretty much as normal.

I remained mobile and fit throughout both pregnancies and, apart from the queasiness on passage, generally felt amazing. I continued to helm, adjust sails, do all the stuff that I usually did. I made some adjustments as my bump grew and my centre of gravity shifted, and I avoided certain activities that might not be so good for the baby. For instance, my usual method of getting back onboard when I'm swimming or diving is to haul myself over the side and into the tender. But it didn't feel right to push my belly against the side like that. Instead, I hauled in at the tender stern, using the underwater parts of the outboard as a sort of foothold to help me step up and in.

I continued to do all the things I was comfortable doing and had been doing for years, including spearfishing. I tried to find scientific studies online about freediving while pregnant, but drew a blank (probably the population of pregnant women who freedive is pretty small). I'd heard anecdotally of a pregnant woman who'd continued to dive to 50m and who gave birth to a healthy baby. But that hardly counted as hard scientific evidence, and I didn't want to risk it. Instead, I did what felt comfortable for me and limited my dives mostly to 5m with the occasional 10m dive. This was quite a lot shallower than I would normally dive and meant I stayed well within my comfortable breath-holding zone.

Elayna *(La Vagabonde II)*

Like me, Hazel remained active and was still windsurfing six months into her first pregnancy. "My sister came to visit us in the British Virgin Island," she recalls. "I was teaching her how to windsurf, but she kept doing it wrong, dropping the sail and getting blown farther out to sea. I was on the beach on my own, thinking 'my sister's going to get blown out to sea and never come back.' I ended up swimming out to her, half-climbing on the board and sort of swimming-sailing the two of us back to shore. As we were making our way to shore, I was thinking 'this is a bit silly.' I couldn't properly climb onto the board because of my bump."

The point is, on the one hand, if you and your growing baby are healthy, then pregnancy should not be treated as an illness and you should carry on being as active as normal, while making adjustments to accommodate your changing body and your precious cargo. On the other hand, this is not a time to challenge yourself or to suddenly take up a new and demanding physical activity. Research the safety of your favorite activities during pregnancy, talk to your obstetrician and/or midwife (more on those below), stay well within your comfort zone, and stay active. I remained on *La Vagabonde II* until I was 32 weeks pregnant with Lenny, continuing to do pretty much everything right up to the end.

Antenatal appointments

When I was newly pregnant with Lenny, I knew I should attend appointments for various scans and tests, but I had no idea what they were or when I should have them. I remember Googling 'What is the pregnancy schedule?' but that didn't give me any definitive answers! Ante-natal care differs from country to country and I found it all confusing and overwhelming. As a first-time mom, I was anxious to do everything I needed for my baby's health and welfare. How was I, an Australian citizen, cruising around the Caribbean on a boat, and not resident in any country, supposed to follow an ante-natal monitoring regime?

Then, I discovered something remarkable. I could hire a private midwife in Australia who would guide me through the whole process! Riley and I weren't on our own. I found a registered midwife through a friend of a friend. However, I now know that there is an entire community of private registered midwives out there, which you'll find online or by calling your regional hospital and asking for a recommendation[5]. For AU$5,500 (~US$3,600), my midwife provided care and guidance throughout the pregnancy, including through labor and birth, and for six weeks post-partum providing, among other things, breastfeeding support. We followed the Australian healthcare system standard for consultations and referrals and for quality and safety. Over the course of the pregnancy, we had ten virtual visits and she was on call 24/7.

She (virtually) held my hand the whole way, helping me to choose clinics in Caribbean islands and the US where I could have scans and tests. We worked as a team. I did the on-the-ground or online research of potential clinics, sent her my findings, and acted on her recommendations. I emailed her the results of each scan which she then discussed with me at our next virtual visit. Although she was on the other side of the world, she provided continuity of care that gave me peace of mind, confidence, and the green light to try a natural home birth in a birthing pool.

Despite her incredible support, Riley and I still had to do the legwork of walking into clinics on our own to request antenatal tests. Most healthcare staff were surprised that I wasn't having regular checkups with my own doctor. Almost every appointment I attended was in a different country, each with a different healthcare system and a different culture of antenatal care. I often felt judged

---

5   For emotional, informational, and physical support at all stages of and after your pregnancy, there are also many professional doulas who will work with you virtually. However, it's important to remember that, while doulas can offer incredible support, they are not required to have the medical training or to provide the medical care of midwives.

by healthcare professionals for not having a dedicated doctor to look after me and for living what they thought was a dangerous lifestyle. They were often shocked that I couldn't immediately tell them the results of my previous tests. I'd nervously reply, "I'll have to look through my emails to find the last test results." Sometimes it feels like everyone's out to make mums feel bad.

I learned a lot during those nine months. When I was pregnant with Darwin, we opted for fewer midwifery services. I felt more confident and knew my pregnant body better, so had fewer virtual visits, fewer scans, and a shorter period of post-natal care, for a fee of AU$2,500 (~US$1,600).

In many countries, including Australia, antenatal, birthing unit, and post-natal care are free through the public health service. In the UK and certain European countries, home births are also free of charge. We chose to keep sailing throughout both pregnancies, which came at the financial cost of hiring the private midwife. A less expensive option might have been to not have a midwife, but to limit our cruising to a smaller area and have all my antenatal appointments in one place, which would have ensured continuity of care in the private health service of one country.

Hiring a midwife didn't even cross Hazel's mind. She and Dave were cruising down the east coast of Canada and the US to the Caribbean during her first pregnancy. A doctor in a clinic in Canada was horrified to discover that Hazel was travelling on a boat. She asked the doctor what tests she needed: "She told me to go for a scan at five months. That was all." By five months, *Ros Ailither* was in US waters. "I didn't realize that you can't just walk into a clinic in the US if you're not already registered with a doctor there," Hazel says, recalling the culture shock of having lived all her life with the British National Health Service. "So, I couldn't access antenatal care." Someone suggested that she have her five-month scan at a clinic for pregnant teenagers. Having completed the scan at the walk-in clinic, a member of staff led Hazel to a different room and asked if Dave beat her up. "I guess they had to ask that to all the teen mums who showed up," Hazel shrugs. "We wanted to pay for the scan, but I just didn't know how or where to access services and no-one seemed to offer them, so the teen pregnancy clinic seemed like the only option." From there, they sailed to Bermuda, their ultimate destination the British Virgin Islands, where they planned to have the baby.

Giving birth
The big 'where' question

Deciding where to have your baby is a consideration that many cruising parents face. There are the health and safety concerns, of course, the issue of giving birth in a place where you feel comfortable and protected and, if you choose a non-hospital birth, knowing that you will have access to hospital or emergency care if needed. There is also the question of post-natal care and how you feel about different cultures of care. While some health care systems insist on immediate skin-on-skin bonding, actively promote breastfeeding, and include dads and other family members as integral to post-natal care, other countries have highly medicalized birth and post-natal cultures, where baby is quickly placed in a nursery with other babies, and the focus is entirely on the mother and/or baby at the expense of the dad or wider family unit (I'm looking at you, South Korea).

And then there is the question of your baby's nationality, the ease with which you can apply for a passport, and the challenge of getting a visa for your baby for the country in which it has been born, if required. Cruising expectant parents need to do a lot of birth research to make the best decisions for the inevitable moment, some months down the line, when the baby decides to arrive. So, get planning early. Figure out if your cruising plans fit with your birthing plans. Familiarize yourself with the procedures for giving birth in your country of choice, including financial costs, type of labor and post-natal care, registering your baby, and so on. But beware! Even the best laid birth plans are often scrapped with the reality of the situation hits!

When I found out I was pregnant, we already had a plan in place to sail to the US to have some work done on the boat and, from there, to the Bahamas. Given the timings, we imagined the baby would be born in the US. I was determined to have a drug free birth and, ideally, a water birth. I discussed all of this with my midwife, she and I researched some birthing centers and, in June, Riley and I toured a few. They all looked fantastic, with amazing facilities and standards of care. They were all free, which was incredible. However, if, during or after labor, either the baby or I had to transfer to hospital, we were looking at potential hospital bills of US$10,000–$20,000. After reassessing our plans, we decided to fly home to Australia. Apart from the cost of flying half way around the world, we knew our public health care would be free, and I could give birth in the comfort of a friend's home, with family and friends nearby.

Hazel's plans to have her baby in the British Virgin Islands were quickly scrapped when she came face-to-face with that country's maternity care. "We did a tour of the hospital," Hazel recalls, "and it was really very basic. There was only one labor room. It had sticky tape on the floor at the entrance, which we were told was to catch the germs as you went in. We weren't convinced." Hazel and Dave soon discovered that, owing to the country's lack of adequate emergency care, an emergency during or after labor would require transfer to the US Virgin Islands by helicopter, the cost of which was beyond their means. Reassessing their options, they sailed to St. Martin, hoping to give birth in the French half of the island and, thus, in the EU, at a cost of about £2000 (approximately US$4000 at the time). By now, Hazel had decided she wanted a home birth, which is not allowed in France or its dependencies. A doctor on St. Martin recommended that she return to England. "The doctor did a test that they don't do in the UK and found that the baby was likely to arrive early." Dropping everything to prepare for the early arrival of the baby, they flew back to the UK when Hazel was seven months pregnant, at the latest date at which she was allowed to fly. Katie was born two weeks after her due date. So much for that test!

Carola had a much easier decision to make, as she and Teddy were in Carola's adopted country of the Netherlands during her pregnancy. However, the couple still had to decide where she would give birth. "In Holland, they really promote giving birth at home," Carola says. "But I was afraid that our midwife would say no to a home birth on a boat, because it wasn't a house and it wasn't sterile." The midwife, however, had no objections to the planned location. "Wherever the baby is made, it can be born," she told Carola and Teddy, reassuring them that the baby would be used to the bacteria in its home environment. The midwife visited the boat, which was in a dock in Amsterdam, was reassured that Carola could quickly transfer off the boat in case of an emergency, and gave her the green light for the home birth she wanted.

Birth stories

My story

At 32 weeks, we were in back in Australia, with a few weeks to spare to get everything organized for the arrival of the baby. I took a hypnobirthing class, hired a birthing pool, and set it up at my friend's AirB&B property that we were renting for the duration. My friend was fine with us setting up the birthing pool, so long as it was in the lounge and that we didn't ruin the carpet or curtains. Did she think I was having the baby from Alien?! I assigned Riley birthing videos to watch, so he'd know what to expect and my virtual midwife was with me in real life. Of course, nothing turned out as planned. Hypnobirthing didn't work for me and as my labor dragged on, I eventually transferred to hospital and was given an epidural. Riley never watched the birthing videos I'd assigned him so, when Lenny was pulled out of me by ventouse after 35 hours of labor, with his head distorted into the shape of a cone, Riley went white as a ghost. The midwife tried to reassure him by revealing that she'd been born by ventouse and, look, wasn't her head shaped just fine! While it

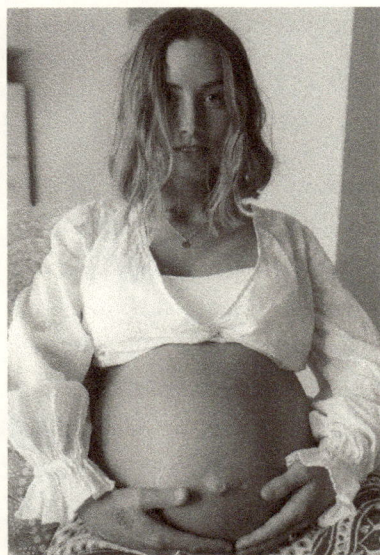

wasn't quite the natural birth I had planned, I was happy that I had given it my all and that I was able to transfer to the safe hands of an obstetrician when I had to.

When I became pregnant again in 2020, I decided to have the baby in the hospital where Lenny was born. Like most mums, I felt much more prepared and confident the second time around.

Elayna *(La Vagabonde II)*

Hazel's story

"I was born at home, so it was nice to carry on that tradition with my own children," Hazel says. Having raced back from the Caribbean, expecting the early arrival of their baby, she and Dave settled into a friend's house, where Katie was born without complications two weeks after her due date. Three years later, when Hazel was pregnant again, they were back in UK waters and, this time, the home birth was aboard *Ros Ailither*. In preparation for the big day, community midwives came to inspect the boat. Dave took them by dinghy from Topsham Quay, across the River Exe, to where *Ros Ailither* was moored. "They were really excited about delivering a baby in such an unusual place," Hazel recalls. "One of them owned a camper van, so she was really game for it, and the rest of them, well, they were the home birthing team, so they'd assisted mums in some unusual places." However, they refused to attend a birth in the middle of the river, in case transfer to hospital was required. "So, we tied *Ros Ailither* alongside the quay. We had to make a special gang plank in case I needed to be carried off," Hazel says. "It was all lovely. My mum was with me, as she had been when Katie was born. She was really great. And Reuben was born right there, alongside Topsham Quay."

Carola's story

"Ellen was born in January," Carola says. "In the days before, a lot of snow had fallen and the day before she was born, I made a big snow bunny on the dock next to the boat. In the morning, I felt that my water had broken, but I didn't want to wake Teddy, because I thought it might be many hours yet. By the afternoon, the frequency of the pain had increased and I sent Teddy to buy formula, in case I wouldn't be able to breastfeed. A few weeks earlier, we had installed central heating in the boat, so it was nice and cozy and the shower was warm. Like many mums, I had nested in the days leading up to the birth, and the boat was 20 times cleaner than usual. I'd packed a

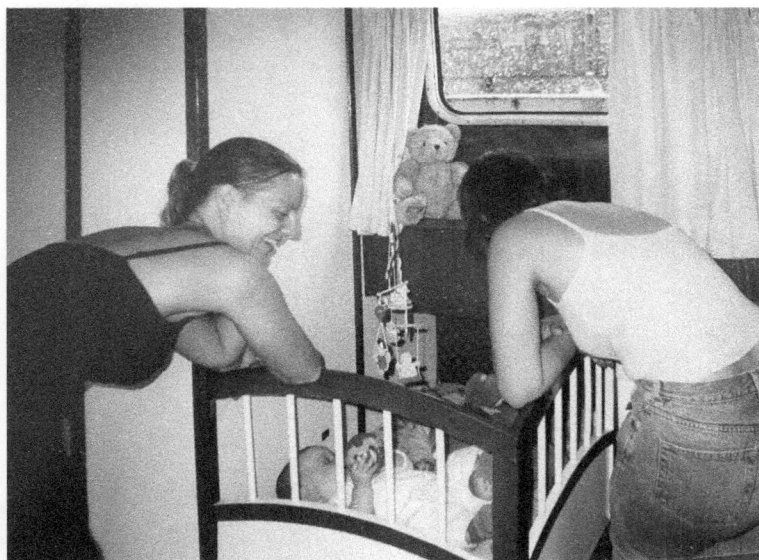

Have baby, will travel *(Maes)*

hospital bag just in case. At 10pm, the midwife came and Ellen was born an hour later. It wasn't perfectly straightforward; at one point the contractions weakened and I didn't seem to be progressing. They nearly decided to transfer me to the hospital, but then Teddy saw the baby's head. 'Come on out,' he said to her and a few minutes later she was wrapped up in her banana leaf basket on top of the washing machine and I was in the shower, barely even aware that I'd had a baby. I kept my hand inside the basket that whole first night and she wrapped her little hand around my finger."

Three and a half years later, Timmy was born, also at home on *Maes*. However, this time, Carola almost didn't make it back across the North Sea from the UK in time. "I wanted to give birth in Holland, because that is where our midwife was. I certainly didn't want to give birth in the middle of the North Sea!" She and Teddy set out from England on a sunny day on a passage back to the Netherlands. By the middle of the night, the weather and sea state had turned for the worse and they made the decision to turn

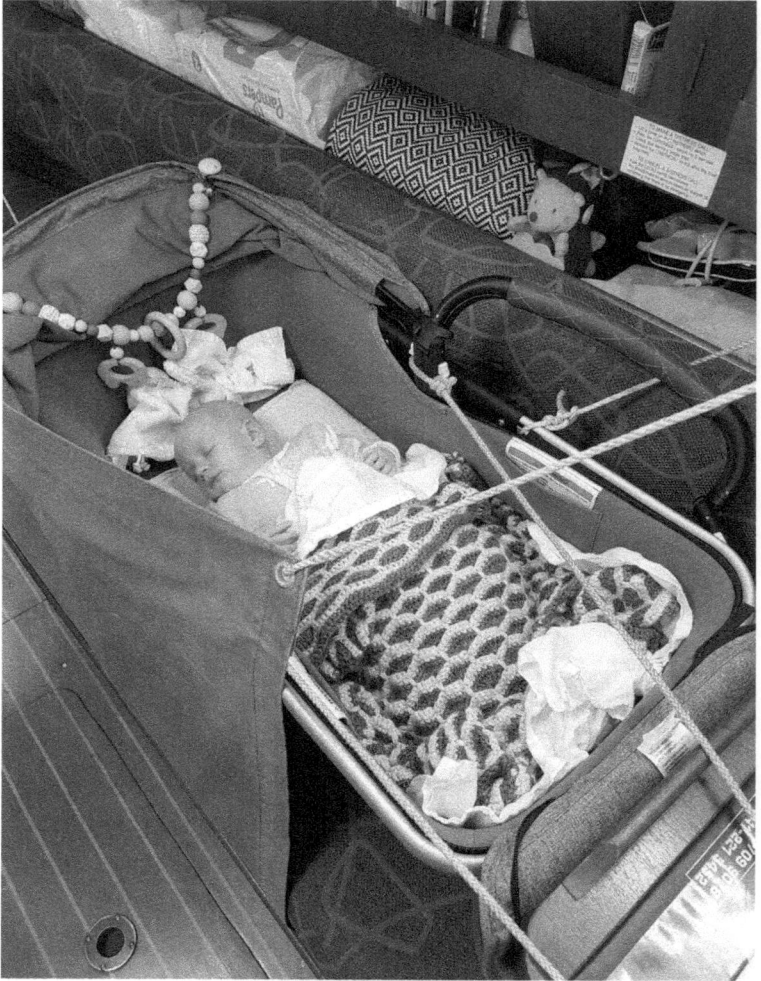

Baby Liz *(Tranquillity)*

around rather than attempt to go on. "We headed back to England and anchored in the same spot that we had left 24 hours earlier." Ten days later, and with the baby's arrival immanent, another weather window appeared and they set out again, this time enjoying a calm and uneventful crossing. "We arrived in port in the middle of Sail Amsterdam, a huge sailing event with all sorts of sailing vessels, including tall ships. We found a space on the dock, rafted to six other boats and with helicopters constantly flying overhead filming footage of the event. Boats were coming and going all the time, bands playing, music all around. Timmy was born in the middle of it all. People constantly walked over our deck to get to their boats. One of our neighbors made a sign that read 'Walk calm – newborn baby on board.' It wasn't a long labor, and I felt quite fit and well afterwards, just as I had with Ellen. After Timmy was born, everyone went to the harbor to enjoy the festivities. I was left onboard with the new baby – I remember being unhappy about that!"

Ellen and Timmy weren't the only ones to be born on the bed in Carola and Teddy's cabin. A few years later, the family's black Labrador, Lily, gave birth to a litter of puppies in the same place. It was clearly a comfortable place for mums of all species!

Bringing baby home

After Lenny was born, I needed time to recover. I had stitches and, to be honest, I tried to do too much, not realizing how much being a new mum takes out of you. I wasn't getting enough sleep (what new mum does?) and when Lenny was only three weeks old, we went on a road trip to shoot a film for South Australia Tourism. My body was under so much stress that I wasn't making enough milk, and Lenny screamed with hunger all the time. It was very tough.

It's quite easy to get a passport in Australia, if you're a citizen, and we applied for Lenny's passport pretty quickly. His passport photo was hilarious – he barely looked human! It was time to go home to *La Vagabonde II*, which was in North Carolina. We applied for a US visa for Lenny so we could pick the boat up and set sail for the Bahamas, where his visa for that country would be issued upon arrival.

Lenny was seven weeks old when we brought him home. We were both quite relaxed about it all. I can still see Lenny slung

Riley and baby Lenny *(La Vagabonde II)*

over Riley's shoulder, with barely enough clothes on, for his first international flight. And how did we adapt to life with a tiny baby on board? I'll tell you all about that in the next chapter.

Top tips

- Conduct antenatal research about the prevalence of diseases (e.g., Zika virus, chicken pox) in your cruising grounds that could put you or your baby at risk. Get up-to-date information from official sources and make adjustments accordingly, which may include altering sailing plans, avoiding certain places, or insect-proofing yourself and/or your boat.

- Hire a private midwife to provide continuity of care from a distance.

- Take on crew. An extra crew member can take up the sailing slack from tired and maybe nauseous mum-to-be. Consider the more emotional characteristics you are looking for in prospective crew; female crew might be more supportive.

- Do post-natal research in advance, so you are prepared for your baby's arrival. Research your baby's passport and visa requirements and the length of application processes. Familiarize yourself with postnatal care, including test and inoculation regimens in the first weeks, and how to complete these if you are already on the move.

- Go home: Consider the emotional, social, financial, and practical benefits of having the baby in your home country. Going home means being cared for in a maternity care culture that you are familiar with, surrounded by the people who love you, with access to your favorite comfort foods. Registering your baby's birth and applying for a passport will also be easier if done in the country where you are already a citizen.

- Prepare for things not to go to plan: A particular country's maternity care may not be what you had expected, you may encounter health difficulties during your pregnancy, your baby may decide to arrive early, your carefully thought-out birth plan will probably not be worth the paper it's written on. Babies don't give a nappy-full of poop about your plans. Just accept it and go with the flow.

Chapter 3

Babies and toddlers

When Lenny and Darwin were babies, we often met cruisers who'd say, "We wouldn't dare sail with such little ones." A lot of people are scared of the idea of having very young children onboard or think it's going to be too difficult. The first few months of sailing with a baby are no tougher than having a baby anywhere else. It's when they start to roll about and crawl that the fun begins!

Life with a baby or toddler is challenging no matter where you live. Like many land-based new parents, new sailing parents are often far from family, friends, and community support networks. On top of that, marketers make you think you can't live without expensive baby kit that is unsuitable for the tight and sometimes leaning spaces aboard a boat. But cruising parents are innovative when it comes to finding their community and creating safe and comfy spaces aboard our homes. So, let's find out how to make those early years a piece of cake and how to dispel your (and your mum's) fears about sailing with very young children.

Two rules to live by
Rule one: Slow down
The most consistent piece of advice from all the parents who've contributed to this book is SLOW DOWN. Over the years, we've met young families who have attempted to carry on sailing just as

they did before the kids came along. Some adapt. Many give up. Life with a small child is a whole lot easier if you simply slow down and adjust your sailing plans to accommodate family life.

I heard about a couple with a three-year-old and a baby under one who planned to circumnavigate the globe in a year and a half. It's doable, of course. François Gabart did it single-handed in 42 days. But we're not here to break records. We're here to have a good time, live a meaningful life, have adventures, and make memories with our children. The couple's plan was ambitious, even without kids. What happened? The mum was seasick so much that by the time they had sailed 2000 NM of mostly coastal waters, they decided to knock their 1.5-year circumnavigation on the head as a failure and return home.

Here's the thing. It's not uncommon for the mums of young children to experience seasickness. Why? Well, as Martina recalls, "I rarely got to helm. I was on mum duty most of the time – changing Katie's nappy, helping Lily use the toilet, preparing snacks, nap time, post-nap time. I felt queasy simply from being below deck attending to the girls' needs."

I can empathize. The queasiness during my pregnancy continued to a lesser extent after we brought Lenny home. Looking back, I think it was a combination of the anxiety of being a new mum and caring for a new baby on a moving boat. Like many cruising families, our roles were heavily gender defined – I did most of the practical side of parenting, while Riley got on with the sailing. So, I was below deck, head down, changing nappies, feeding Lenny. No wonder I felt queasy.

Bart remembers being on the helm in the North Sea in a little too much swell with Kim below deck, feeding Liz. He watched, anxious and distressed, as Kim stood up, walked to the galley, holding Liz in one arm while steadying herself with the other, and vomited into the sink. The things we put ourselves through. For no good reason. You don't need to push yourself like that when you've got a small new human to look after. Take it easy. Listen to your body.

Back to our wannabe circumnavigators. It's quite likely that mum was seasick simply because they were pushing themselves to sail vast distances in a short period of time, trying to meet self-imposed goals and deadlines. They might still be at sea if they'd simply been kind to themselves, slowed down, and cruised at a family-friendly pace. Who knows, they might even have circumnavigated by now, but in three or five or seven years, rather than in one and a half. Ask yourself if you really need to achieve those sailing goals right now, or ever? Perhaps you'll have just as great a time, or better, if you relax, take the pressure off, use your time to delve more deeply into the places you visit, and enjoy being with your kids as they grow, learn, and explore.

Of course, it's not always possible to take it slowly. Hazel and Dave brought Katie home to *Ros Ailither* at the tender age of two weeks and she was sailing for the first time three weeks later. "She was born in mid-April," Hazel says, "So, by the time we got back to *Ros Ailither* in St Martin, it was getting close to hurricane season and we had to get moving. We didn't want to do anything silly with a new baby on board, so we hot footed it to Bermuda." A friend joined them to provide practical and moral support. "She probably saw me at my worst," Hazel laughs, "With a brand-new baby and with the worst weather we had ever encountered."

Jessica and Jeroen also started life aboard at a fast pace, when Benjamin and Frank were three and two years old. Their budget didn't stretch to spending a lot of time in marinas, so they sailed hard into the wind from the Netherlands to northern Spain, a passage with few suitable anchorages. "That first month was stressful and I kept thinking, 'Is this really it?'" Jessica recalls. Long passages, no more than a night or two in one place, and the hard grind of planning, navigating, and being constantly alert clashed with the needs of the children. Unhappy children made for unhappy sailing.

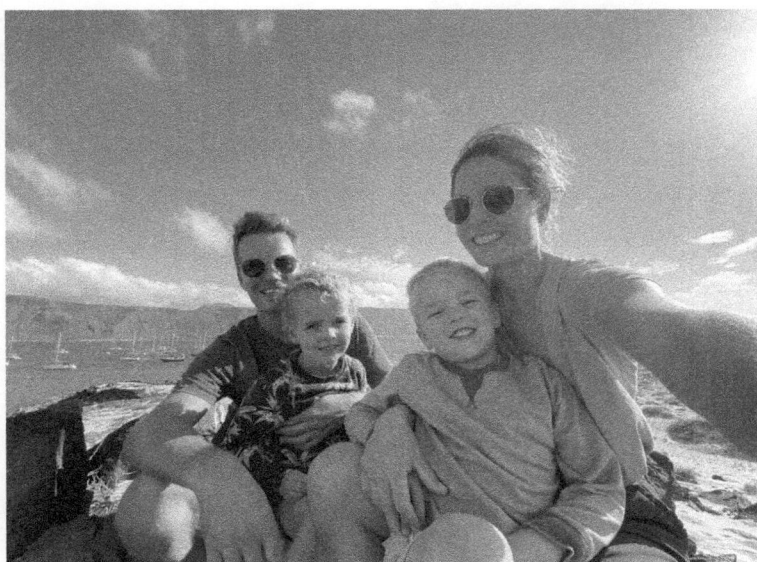

Jeroen, Frank, Benjamin and Jessica (*Sans Souci*)

When they reached northern Spain, they slowed down at last. "We started enjoying it," says Jeroen. "For the kids, it was more fun. We went to the beach and climbed rocks and watched fish. It felt more like the life we had been looking for." The family has now made a conscious effort to slow down. "Cruising is much easier when you live your life at a pace that works for your children," Jeroen says. He's right. What's the rush? Do you really need to accomplish some sailing goal by your self-imposed deadline?

Slowing down means managing your expectations for how many nautical miles you're going to get under your belt. Shorter passages and day sails are much more practical. They take the pressure off the caregiving parent (in most cases, the mum) and off the parent who is, effectively, now a single-handed sailor. For us, the Bahamas was a great place to cruise with small children. With islands often so close together that you can see your next anchorage from the current one, short to medium day sails became the norm for us.

Slowing down also means managing your expectations for what you will do when you go ashore. Bart says, "Unlike cruisers with older kids, we aren't able to do as much exploring on land – no big hikes, no travelling some place in a bus for five hours." Remember, this phase in your child's life is short-lived. So, make the most of those days digging sand on the beach, or going for short hikes with your baby or toddler strapped to your body. As time passes, and kids become stronger and more capable, you and they can do more. I can't believe how much more we can do as a family than we could even a year ago.

Rule two: Establish routines

Many of us choose a cruising life to escape the 9 to 5 (make that 5am to 9pm) routine, and the daily grind of life on land. Few things in life match the freedom of living on a boat, being your own boss, and travelling where the wind and currents take you.

But here's the thing – kids love routine. They crave it. They start to go a little crazy when they don't have it. From the moment they're born, they're learning new things every day. The world is full of wonder and newness. And while that's exciting, it's also exhausting and scary. Routine, however, is stabilizing, reassuring, and calming. Creating routines around feeding, bathing, and sleep times for younger children is extremely important. For boat kids, the world around their home changes sometimes every day. They go to sleep in one anchorage or one country and wake up in another. They made some great friends yesterday, but they're preparing to set sail today and may never see them again. In the face of such dramatic changes, routine in your daily life at home is essential. Indeed, throughout this book, you'll see that routine is the key to a happy sailing life for kids of all ages. Start as you mean to go on, and create routines with your baby or toddler.

Cruising life can be hectic at times. There's always something going on, so much to do, so much we *want* to do. But no matter what, we try to maintain a routine that, for the boys, includes regular mealtimes, morning time off the boat with either Riley or me when we're on anchor, regular nap times, hanging out together as a family in the afternoon, and evening and bedtime routines. Even when the boys were tiny, no matter how busy we were with them or with work, Riley and I always committed to giving each other some routine space each day too. Ok, ok, so we're not perfect. Those routines get broken sometimes, and that's when we realize how much calmer and happier the boys are when we stick to them.

Of course, you shouldn't be a slave to those routines either. Routines evolve over time, as your children grow and develop, and anchorage routines may differ quite a bit from passage routines. We even like to take regular big breaks from our cruising life to reset our internal clocks, have some reflection time, gain a different perspective on what we're doing in our lives, and assess our life goals. So, every three months or so, we move ashore, usually into a rented house or to stay with friends. This break in routine has always been disruptive for the boys. We inevitably forget some favorite toy and they are away from the familiarity of home. But this hybrid approach to our cruising life is important for our mental health and our relationship. We've found that it generally takes about two weeks for the boys to adjust to their new environment, to fall into a new routine, and to start to really enjoy it.

I won't tell you what your liveaboard routine should be. That's up to you, to be created and shaped around the needs of your family. I'll simply say this: create a routine, stick to it, but change it if it's not working, and adapt it to meet the needs of your growing children and your evolving family life.

Life on board

What you need on board

Marketers of baby products would have you believe that your baby requires a houseful of baby-specific furniture and other kit. That's simply not feasible on most boats. The truth is, your baby needs very little. We cruisers are an adaptable lot, and we've found some ingenious ways to keep our little ones happy and safe onboard.

What does your baby actually need? Somewhere to sleep. A means of transportation. Somewhere to sit and look around at the world. Safe spaces to crawl and learn to walk. Some materials to help them learn, develop, and enjoy themselves.

My top 8 essential baby items

See my video at https://www.youtube.com/watch?v=oWqIDscVfdY where I review the following essential baby items and how we couldn't live without them when the boys were babies:

- Jolly jumper
- Baby carrier
- Sturdy feeding chair that attached directly to the table
- Bassinet
- Nappies – bamboo if cloth is too difficult
- Hand held food blender
- Nappy/work bag
- Life jacket

Carrying and moving around

The number one piece of baby kit is a sling. There are many different styles available, from structured buckle and clip types to natural fabric wraparound and ring sling types. Parent and baby groups often run free workshops where you can try out different styles. A sling can be useful when it's time for boat maneuvers and it's a favorite place for many babies. "One of us would be behind the wheel," Bart says, "with Liz strapped to our chest. That way, we had both hands free. Liz was content and didn't make a scene while we got on with the business of maneuvering the boat." However, be aware of the dangers of carrying your baby in a sling. If you fall into the water while making boat maneuvers, you will struggle to keep your head above water, with the weight of your baby on your chest. Consider wearing a slim life-jacket to provide some buoyancy, should you and baby fall in. Alternatively, place baby in a secure seat (see below) so they can see you throughout the maneuver. Slings, and later back carriers for when babies can sit upright, are also extremely useful for getting on with chores and for getting around on land. "It's really helpful when you want to go hiking," Bart says.

Most cruisers avoid strollers. They take up a lot of room, are difficult to get ashore, and often break down owing to the more rugged terrain or unpaved roads in many of the places that we choose to visit. When a front wheel broke off in Gibraltar, Jessica and Jeroen decided not to replace their stroller and to get scooters instead. "Just the normal ones – not electric," Jessica explains. "We bought little steps at a sports and outdoor store, that the kids can stand on." They also have a four-wheeled collapsible trolley that the boys can sit in and in which they can haul groceries. Jeroen advises buying a good quality trolley, as their inexpensive one has proven not very sturdy. While the trolley takes up less space, it is also restricted to better surfaced and urban roads.

Secure seating

Most baby and toddler stores stock feeding chairs that attach to a table. We used them on both inside or outside tables. The cockpit table on *La Vagabonde II* was super sturdy and not too close to the edge of the boat. If a sudden squall blew up and Riley needed me to quickly put in a reef or adjust the sails, I could simply stick Lenny or Darwin into this feeding chair, where he was secure and could see what we were doing. The feeding chair was also a secure place in the saloon when I was cooking and I didn't want him crawling or toddling near the stove. That chair became like another crew member and I used it throughout the toddler stage, when I needed the boys to be secure.

Some cruisers opt to bolt a car seat onto the cockpit, while others prefer more flexible swinging options, using ropes and swinging chairs (see photo of Ellen). The IKEA high chair is a useful piece of adapted kit in this regard. Bart and Kim strapped it with ropes in the companionway, where Liz could reach a small cockpit bench to play with her toys and interact with whichever parent was on the helm. Lenny and Darwin both loved the Jolly Jumper bouncing seat, which we could easily secure inside or in the cockpit. We found that it swung around a lot when the boat was moving, so we only put them in it when we were at anchor.

Remember, no matter what seating you use, always place it under the spray hood or other shelter, to protect your baby from sun, wind, rain, and spray.

Sleeping

A boat can be a noisy place. Sailing, sitting at anchor, even tied up in a marina, can be noisy at times with water rushing against the hull and wind in the rigging, not to mention the noise of everyday life, living in a small space, doing daily home chores and boat maintenance, talking, playing music. From the very beginning, we were determined that the boys would be able to sleep anywhere, with any amount of noise. Now they really can sleep anywhere. In fact, the more noise the better!

If you haven't yet moved aboard with your baby or toddler, I suggest it's time to start making noise! There are all sorts of ways – from white noise machines or a white noise soundtrack on YouTube to putting them down to sleep next to the washing machine. It's harder to create artificial noise once you set sail, because the sources I've mentioned above will quickly drain your boat or phone batteries.

Don't tip-toe around your kids – literally or metaphorically – and they'll soon learn to fall asleep and, critically, stay asleep, no matter what's going on around them. You'll thank me for this when your toddler sleeps peacefully through a 40-knot squall or through every squeak and tap on the rigging when the wind's blowing from just the wrong direction.

La Vagabonde II is an owner's version, with three cabins – one in one hull (where Riley and I slept before Lenny came along) and two in the other. In hindsight, we probably should have moved into the two-cabin hull. That would have allowed all three of us to be together, with Lenny and I in one cabin and Riley just a Sophie the Giraffe's throw away in the other. But that hull was always for guests and we didn't think to change when Lenny arrived. So, I slept in our cabin with baby Lenny in a basinet beside me and Riley slept on the comfy sofa bed in the saloon, which he already used for night watches. When Lenny outgrew the basinet, he slept beside me until

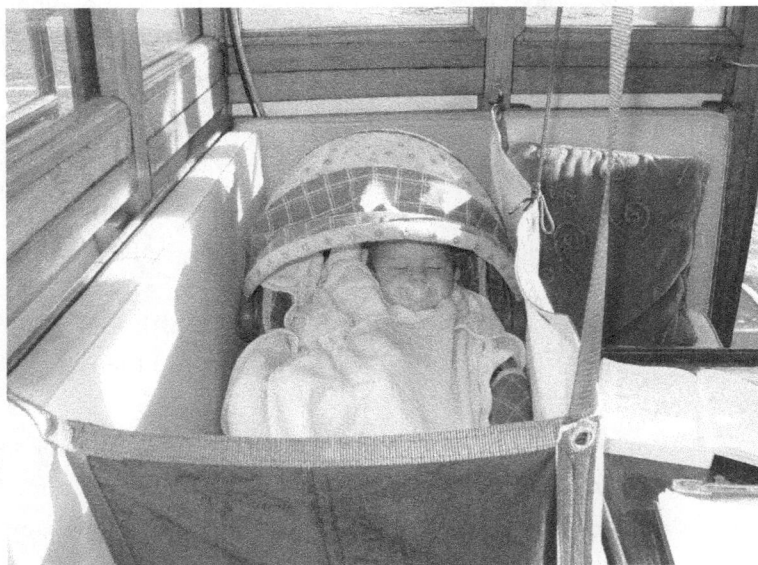

Sleeping *(Ros Ailither)*

he was two and a half. It had its advantages: feeding was easier and our sleep wasn't disturbed too much by the middle-of-the-night needs of a baby.

Many cruising parents of very young children choose to co-sleep. Martina accidentally ended up co-sleeping with Lily and Katie when they first moved aboard *Carina of Devon*. "The forward cabin was going to be the girls' bedroom. But we'd dumped all our stuff there and it was going to take a few days to sort out. So, they slept with me in the aft cabin and Julian slept in the saloon. It was a revelation. They were one and three years old at the time and I hadn't had a decent night's sleep in over three years. They slept soundly beside me that first night, and Julian and I woke up refreshed. So, we carried on like that and they didn't move into their own cabin for a year."

When Darwin arrived, he slept with me, as Lenny had, and Lenny moved out to Riley in the saloon. At first, we were scared he might crawl outside during the night, so we kept the hatches and doors shut. We soon discovered, however, that on the rare occasions when he did wake, he simply sat on the bed and played with whatever toys were to hand. After that, we stopped worrying and put toys within his reach, so he'd have something to play with if he woke up. Every kid is different and, while Lenny had no interest in exploring beyond the bed at night, it's no guarantee that other kids won't. Take precautions if your child has potential access to the cockpit, deck, or potentially unsafe spaces below deck.

These sleeping arrangements worked for us. All four of us slept better when Riley focused on one of the boys and I focused on the other.

Ellen and Timmy slept in banana leaf basinets as babies, graduating into the bed alongside Carola and Timmy after a few months. "We read that after four months you should remove the baby from your bedroom, otherwise they'd be frightened of the things you get up to in there!" Carola laughs. "We prepared a cabin for

Ellen, but it was cozier all together. Every few months, we expanded the bed, regularly adapting it to our changing needs." When Ellen was six, she moved into her own cabin. Timmy decided he wanted his own space too, and his parents created a berth for him in a space in the middle of the boat.

At two months old, Liz slept in a basinet stroller secured in a sea sling in a saloon berth. Now that she's older, she sleeps in *Tranquillity*'s aft cabin in a Deryan tent[6] on top of the bed. This handy, light-weight pop-up travel tent comes in a range of sizes for young children. "It gives her a bit more protection," her mom Kim says. "The aft cabin is quite big, so the tent also gives her more of a sense of having her own space."

Let's face it, we all need to sleep well, and you have to find the sleeping arrangements that best suit you and your family, whether that's co-sleeping as a family, co-sleeping with one parent, or giving your baby or toddler their own space. The right way to do it is the way that works for you and your children and don't let anyone tell you otherwise.

Nappies

We were determined to use cloth nappies with Lenny. After a few weeks, we were defeated by them. Without a washing machine, we washed the nappies the same way we do all our clothes – by soaking them, stamping on them, and scrubbing them when we shower each evening. That didn't work with the nappies which never got fully clean. On top of that, we simply couldn't keep up with the eight or nine nappies Lenny was going through each day. Drying them was the biggest problem. If we left them on the line to dry when we were sailing, they got sprayed with salt water and had to be washed again. And some days it rained. Tied to shore, with access to fresh water

---

6   https://www.deryan.com/en/collections/campingbed

and a washing machine, then cloth nappies are a good option for some. But even with those amenities, they can be a challenge. Carola and Teddy were dissuaded from using cloth owing to the amount of electricity needed to dry them in a dryer during the damp winters in the Netherlands.

If you have a washing machine on board and are cruising in a warmer/dryer part of the world, then I would absolutely recommend cloth nappies for their environmental sustainability. The initial outlay can be expensive (although you can buy them second hand), but you'll save a lot of money over the course of the two or more years your child will wear them.

Our alternative to cloth were disposable biodegradable bamboo nappies. They cost more than plastic nappies and have only limited availability. We didn't buy enough, so when they ran out, we had to buy the regular disposable nappies locally. That broke my heart and I regretted not buying more when we had the chance.

When your baby is going through eight or more disposable nappies a day, you have to consider storage. Used nappies should be stored in cool place, preferably in a lidded container. The anchor locker is a good option. Placing cotton wool with a few drops of tea tree oil in the bottom of the storage container can help to eliminate odors. As soon as you get to shore, dispose of them in the appropriate manner.

Carola suggests a somewhat radical approach – no nappies at all. "Our children attended a play group when they were two years old. The teacher removed all their nappies immediately. Some parents weren't happy, but we were fine. They had regular group bathroom times. Sometimes there were accidents, but mostly they saw others using the potty and learned quickly from that." It's certainly something to consider as you get closer to potty training time.

Toddler safety
Onboard

There are all sorts of ingenious ways to keep your little ones safe when they start to crawl and move around. We used stair gates for the companionways in the saloon to limit access to anywhere where there was a greater likelihood of falling. However, you don't need to buy expensive or bulky kit. Instead, you can adapt and use whatever you have onboard. Kim and Bart placed a table across the door to Liz's cabin so she couldn't get out without assistance and crawl about on the leaning boat. Alternatively, a net barrier hooked in place when your child is sleeping or during play or quiet time, will prevent them from falling out. When Martina and Julian's girls eventually moved to their own cabin, a wooden dinghy seat was placed as a barrier across the top of the berth each night to prevent them from sliding out while asleep.

Putting netting around the guard rails as soon as Lenny started to walk was a game changer. Before that, we jumped up at Lenny's slightest crawl or roll, scared that he'd go overboard. Netting not only keeps your child from falling overboard; it keeps toys, winch handles, and all manner of objects from going in too.

A toddler can be a far more challenging sailing companion than a baby. Katie learned to walk when she was 16 months old, during an Atlantic crossing. "It was much harder than sailing when she was five weeks old," Hazel recalls. Katie spent a lot of that passage in *Ros Ailither*'s large wheelhouse. Her parent had already installed stair gates on the doors. "That way, we could open the doors to let air in, but Katie couldn't get out."

"We had long discussions about safety," Hazel remembers. "We had a cold box on deck and I changed the ice packs every day. I'd take Katie out to help me. We debated whether it was safer for her to be in a life jacket, so that in the extremely unlikely event that she fell in, she'd float away; or to be tethered to me and hope that I didn't fall in." In the end, they went with tethering. "It was much

Crossing the Atlantic
at 17 mos (*Ros Ailither*)

easier to move around on deck that way. We had quite high hand rails, so there was little likelihood she'd fall in."

Familiarize yourself with your boat's accident danger zones from your toddler's perspective and consider the material changes and safety practices you need to put in place. And remember, no matter what, your toddler is going to outsmart you!

Boat to shore

Most of us get from boat to shore by tender. The basic guidelines are simple: (a) Never carry your baby or toddler attached to your body: if you go overboard, the weight of your child in its sling or carrier will pull you under; (b) Never place your baby or toddler in a pram/stroller/baby carrier: if that goes overboard, your baby is sinking to the bottom under its weight; (c) Never attach them by a harness to the tender: if there's an accident, they're attached to it; (d) Always put your baby or toddler in a correctly fitting life jacket and hold on to them while you're in the tender. Hazel wondered for a while whether it was better for Katie to be in a life jacket or in a sling. However, when Hazel fell into the water from the tender, she realized how dangerous it would have been if Katie had been in a sling. "I went straight in. Head under. If she'd been strapped on to me, we'd both have been underwater."

Keep your child safe by slowing down, taking your time, and observing the dangers around you. If the waves are short and choppy, or the wind is up, consider whether the whole family needs to go ashore. If going ashore under those conditions is absolutely necessary, ask yourself if the adult to child ratio is adequate to hold on to those little guys.

Getting on and off your boat with very young children can cause some stress. Before children can walk, it's best practice for an adult on the boat to carefully hand the baby down to an adult in the tender and vice versa. We learned through trial and error not to step between boat and tender while holding the kid – someone once fell in while stepping over and holding Darwin at the same time. Luckily, he was wearing his life jacket. Poor Darwin, he's the butt of all our errors (see below). Passing your baby over even a few centimeters of water can be scary at first, or if sea conditions are poor. Take your time, don't rush it. Getting from boat to tender and back again is now second nature to Lenny and Darwin. Even so, we have non-negotiable rules. Darwin is always picked up and transferred to dock/tender/boat, with another adult ready to take hold of him. Lenny can now do it by himself, but must always hold an adult's hand.

Your toddler's favorite place in the tender will probably be the prow. They'll love the wind on their faces and the speed will make them giggle as they bounce up and down over the waves. This is the absolute *worst* place your kid can be and I advise that you never allow them to be there. If they fall in the water, the only place they're going is under the boat and into the propellor. The sides of the tender are the safest and, if possible, make sure an adult is holding on to them while underway.

Life jackets

Every cruising parent has a different opinion about life jackets. The truth is, neither parents nor children like them. Baby life jackets are particularly badly designed. Cheap or expensive, it doesn't matter. They're bulky and uncomfortable and, as Hazel says, "like a massive shoe box around the baby." But babies who are too young to support their heads, and babies who haven't yet learned to swim should wear life jackets with neck support. Get your baby used to wearing it by letting them float in it in a swimming pool or at the beach. Manufacturers really need to improve the design to make them less bulky and more comfortable.

However, the advice for everyone, no matter what age, is to wear a life jacket in a tender and on a pontoon. Over time you'll get used to your own child and devise your own rules for when they should wear life jackets, such as on deck or when underway. Parents on bigger boats, with more substantial cockpits/wheelhouses, apply the life jacket rule when their kids leave those safe/enclosed spaces.

But I'm going to be completely honest with you. We haven't always been strict with the life jacket rule. When we were in the Bahamas, usually anchored in about two meters of crystal-clear water, we sometimes didn't bother with their jackets, if the water and weather were really calm. One day, when Darwin was one year old, and coming back from the beach with Riley and Lenny, he fell over the side. Luckily, he wasn't at the front of the tender and Riley had the kill cord attached. It only took a split second for Riley to kill the outboard and dive in after him. I was watching from *La Vagabonde II* as Riley dived in and left Lenny alone in the tender. Riley swam slowly and awkwardly back to the tender, struggling a bit, as he hauled Darwin and then himself aboard. A couple of minutes later, all three were back safely aboard *La Vagabonde II* and Darwin was none the worse for it. But Riley and I were badly shaken, thinking about what could have happened if the water had been murky or rough. It was the last time the boys ever went ashore without life jackets. We learned our lesson: no matter how calm or straightforward the tender ride seems, always put your little ones in life jackets. And always use the kill cord. I can't emphasize this enough. The kill cord is a nifty little piece of kit. One end of this short lanyard is connected to the outboard motor and the other

Lifejackets (*Carina of Devon*)

(usually at the wrist or leg) to the person operating the motor. In the event of an accident, a quick tug on the kill cord immediately shuts off the outboard motor. Not having a kill cord can be fatal. There is no excuse not to connect the kill cord every time you use the tender.

When Lenny and Darwin learned to swim, they graduated to comfortable U-shaped jackets with CO_2 canisters for big ocean crossings and water sports buoyancy aids (rather than full on life jackets) for going ashore.

Always put your child's lifejacket on, so that it becomes second nature to them and they will reach for it themselves because they associate it with going ashore or going onto spaces on your boat where life jackets are compulsory. From the age of two, whenever he wanted to go outside, Lenny wouldn't say "Can I go outside?" Instead, he'd ask, "Can I put my life jacket on?"

Every family has a different approach to life jacket use and water safety. But none of those solutions is ideal and it's easy to see the flaws in each. Find what works best for you, and your children, and for the configuration of your boat and your tender. And be consistent in your safety rules and routines.

Life jackets for babies and toddlers

There are lots of websites out there offering advice on the best life jackets for babies and toddlers. Here are three that we've found helpful:

https://www.thebump.com/a/best-infant-life-jackets#2

https://www.whattoexpect.com/baby-products/best-infant-life-jackets/

https://annainthehouse.com/best-baby-life-jackets/

In the water

Teaching your child to swim is one of the greatest gifts you can give them and can also save their lives. Lenny had his first swimming lesson at six months in the Bahamas. At first, he only had five lessons. For the next few months, we practiced what he/we had learned most days. Six months later, we arranged for more lessons.

Because we move around so much, it's hard to find swimming coaches. Spacing out lessons worked really well, because we could practice and solidify what he learned, and properly build on those skills the next time he had lessons. He continued to have occasional lessons until he was two and a half years old. By then, he could doggy paddle and hold his head above water. Unlike most kids, most of Lenny's lessons were in the sea. That was more difficult for him, but it made him more resilient. In between lessons, we'd swim with him from beaches or at swimming pools. We tried swimming with him off the back of the boat, but that was too hard to manage until he was a more confident swimmer.

How do you find swimming lessons for your kid? The hassle of taxis or public transport to get to swimming pools puts a lot of cruising parents off. However, we were surprised to discover how many swimming coaches will actually come to you. Hotels will often let you use their swimming pool for a small fee, which may be more convenient than having to get to a public pool. Ask other sailing families if they want to share lessons. By doubling up, you'll save money, as the coach can give lessons to two or more children at once.

Hazel and Dave spent a winter in a marina in Newport, Rhode Island before Katie turned two. Yachties using the marina had access to a nearby hotel swimming pool. They took Katie to the pool every night. "She absolutely loved it," Hazel says, and started to learn to swim there.

Kim and Bart on *Tranquillity* recommend the Baby Swim Baby Rescue program (other programs include Swim Float Swim and Infant Aquatic; see Resources). They introduced Liz to this technique when she was nine months old. The method teaches young children to rescue themselves if they fall in the water. "She loves the water so much and we don't worry about accidents so much because she is such a confident swimmer now. If she fell in the sea at our anchorage, she has the skills to get herself in the correct position and swim. She would probably find it pretty funny."

Toys and books

Ever been in a home that's bursting at the seams with expensive toys, but the kid's happily playing with a cardboard box or a saucepan? We've skipped the expensive toys part and gone straight for the saucepans. Babies and toddlers require so little, and are content to play with everyday objects around the boat. Sites like Pinterest are jam packed full of great ideas for converting everyday items into toys and games. You don't even need those sites. Kids will just pick things up and play with them. Beware of small parts, toxic chemicals, and other dangers to small children who like to put everything in their mouths.

Riley is a minimalist, so we've been selective with toys and have bought very few over the years. Most of what we have are hand-me-downs from other cruising families. If they're still in good condition when Lenny and Darwin outgrow them, then we pass them on to others. The largest piece of toddler kit we've had onboard was a balance bike, which we bought for Lenny when he was two. He used it a lot when we were ashore on suitable terrain.

Babies and toddlers love books, and it's never too early to start them on their reading adventure. But books are heavy and take up a lot of space. While I recommend digital reading options for older children, the baby and toddler years are the time for big, chunky real books. Our boys loved the images and the tactility of flip books and the Usborne *That's not my...* series. Don't forget to visit the children's section of libraries in places you visit. It doesn't matter if you can't read the language – just tell your own story from the pictures.

Meal time

Breastfeeding and formula

It goes without saying that breastfeeding is the easiest way to feed your baby while cruising. You can do it anytime and anywhere and don't need any kit. I breastfed Lenny until he was four months old, but my milk supply was low, so I had to introduce formula. We were in the US, and I had access to great organic formula. Before setting sail, we stocked up on about ten tins. That was a bad idea, because they reached their expiry date faster than Lenny got through them. In the following months, whenever crew or family joined us via the US, they bought formula en route. That was inconvenient for everyone, but I was wary of the limited formula options in the Bahamas, containing poorer quality ingredients.

Formula, no matter what the brand, comes with water quality and safety concerns. The *La Vagabonde II* water maker produced exceptionally good quality water. However, in the absence of a water maker, the US Centers for Disease Control recommends making tap water safe by boiling or disinfecting it[7]. When considering your baby-feeding options, bear in mind (a) availability of formula in your cruising grounds, (b) expiry dates, and (c) water quality.

My milk was in full flow for Darwin and he breastfed until he was two years old. That made life easier all around. My lesson learned and my advice: breastfeed for as long as you can.

Weaning and first solid food

Good quality food is obviously the best option for weaning your baby. In many countries, vegetables, fruits, meat, and fish are readily available. For example, municipal markets in many parts of Europe, Africa, and Asia offer a staggering choice of inexpensive fresh plant foods, from which you can make hearty first meals. However, some parts of the world offer fewer options. The boys were both weaned in the Bahamas, where the supply of locally-produced fresh fruit and vegetables is limited. Therefore, before setting sail, we stocked up on tiny tins of good quality weaning meals, such as mashed potatoes and carrots, or banana, mango, and oats. If the boys had been weaned elsewhere, then I would certainly have made most of the meals myself.

I try to get fresh vegetables into the boys every day, with steamed vegetables and rice being a common family dinner. Because boat refrigerators don't stay very cold and we do all our shopping on foot, we tend to shop for smaller quantities of fresh produce every couple of days.

---

7   https://www.cdc.gov/nutrition/infantandtoddlernutrition/formula-feeding/
     infant-formula-preparation-and-storage.html

Katie, 3,
Reuben, 2 mos
(Ros Ailither)

Sailing babies and toddlers

Very young children require very little to keep them happy and healthy. They just want to be where you are. So, make the time to be with them too and explore the fascinating world from their perspective.

Tips

- Slow down: Don't set unrealistic milage or exploring goals; instead, adjust your pace and enjoy the world from your baby's or toddler's perspective.

- Creating routines will reassure and ground your small child and will help to create space for care, work, and fun.

- Simplify what you have on the boat: Your baby or toddler needs very little. Keep paraphernalia to a minimum and repurpose items you already have onboard. This phase in their lives is very short, and things will soon be obsolete.

- Teach your child to swim: For pleasure, for safety, for a lifetime of incredible experiences, give your child the gift of swimming.

- Familiarize yourself with the danger points on your boat from the perspective of your small child and take steps to mitigate those dangers.

Chapter 4

The pre-school years

Those baby and toddler days already feel like a lifetime ago. With each new phase of Lenny and Darwin's lives, our cruising life evolves too. They are becoming more sociable outside of our little family unit, and their world is expanding as they make friends with other children and with trusted adults. Those early years of childhood, from around three to six or seven years, are when your kid's world typically starts to expand beyond the immediate family. It's a time for play and fun, socialization, and developing friendships. We explore all those things in this chapter, as well as sharing some tips for maintaining contact with family and friends back home. Children take their first steps into education at this stage, and it is a time when cruising parents start to think about education options, so some of the other parents and I will explain what early years education looks like for our families.

Many couples decide to set sail when their kids are in this age bracket. Children are more mobile and capable. They can go on short to medium family hikes, are more inclined to endure longer trips on public transport, and are interested in literally everything. They're also a clean slate and are far more adaptable to new environments than older children. For families from countries where formal education is compulsory (including many European countries), these few years offer a window of freedom and opportunity to cruise without falling foul of the education system. Even for parents who are not expected to conform to formal education requirements, many lack confidence in home educating their children past the ages of six or seven. I'll dive deeper into education options for older children in Chapters 5 and 6.

Socializing

If you're not yet a liveaboard, you might be forgiven for thinking that it's a solitary life. Sure, there are times when you don't see anyone else for weeks on end – an ocean crossing, for example, or if you decide to spend time somewhere really remote. But, for the most part, the cruising life, while very independent, is also very sociable. Most cruisers follow annual wind and weather patterns, choose the same anchorages because they're sheltered and the holding is good, and favor those parts of the world that are equipped for and welcoming to liveaboards. So, it makes sense that there's a strong sense of community among cruisers. And that community is just like any other. You'll meet people who are super sociable and others who prefer their own company. You'll meet solo sailors and families. You'll meet sailors young and old, those who've just set sail on their first boat, and others who've been on the sea for fifty years.

By the age of three or so, children have started to socialize beyond the confines of their immediate family, and the opportunities to get to know people of all ages, from all sorts of backgrounds, and in all sorts of contexts, seems almost endless.

Cruising community

If you sail even for a short while, you'll soon start to feel part of the community. Because that's what cruising life is – a moving, morphing, continuously evolving community. You might meet a retired Canadian couple somewhere on the south coast of England. You'll have a few meals together, enjoy a bottle of wine, go for walks, help each other out with boat chores. Then you'll sail off in different directions. Two years later, you'll rock up at an anchorage in the Bahamas and there they are. You resume your friendship, catching up on where you've been and what you've been getting up to. They'll be amazed at how much your children have grown, and your children, at first shy around these strangers, will soon warm to them all over again. Six months later, you'll bump into them again in North Carolina. Along the way, they'll introduce you to their cruising friends and you'll introduce them to yours, and your web of connections will grow.

One of the great joys of meeting other liveaboards in this way, and living in an ever-changing community, is the support and help that we offer each other, including emotional support and help with childcare. Once your children are in that three to six age range, they start to spread their wings a little and develop friendships with other cruisers. And while I'm certainly not advocating handing your kids over to the first cruisers you befriend along the way, you will now and again make friendships about which both you and your children are extremely comfortable.

Martina and Julian's daughters were five and six years old when they met fellow cruisers, Claire and Ed. "We were overwintering in the same place and we got to know them over a few months," Martina says. "They were a retired couple, with three adult sons back in the UK, but no grandchildren yet. Our girls really liked Claire and she liked them. So, when she offered to babysit so we could go on a date, we jumped at her offer." Over the years, Martina met a few older cruisers with whom she and her daughters felt comfortable. "Often, older sailors miss their own grandchildren back home, and are only too happy to help you with your kids. If they want to be temporary grandparents to my children, and my children are happy with that, then we go for it."

Bart and Kim also accept help from other cruisers. "We've made some lovely friends who really enjoy babysitting and who Liz is very comfortable with. About once a month we have the luxury of

Lily and Katie *(Carina of Devon)*

doing something together for a whole day, while our friends take care of Liz."

Maybe you're thinking, 'yikes, I'm not leaving my kids with strangers.' First of all, they won't be strangers. I'm talking about people who have already become your trusted friends. And second, I'm not suggesting you do anything that makes you feel uncomfortable. Maybe you'll never feel comfortable leaving your children alone with other people. But giving them unmediated time with others – for walks, picnics, days on the beach – will be an immense gift to your kids. The cruising community is full of amazing, kind, capable, interesting people of all ages who will welcome you and your children. My advice: do what feels comfortable and safe for you and your children.

Finding other cruising families

This type of friendship-making is even more likely to happen with other cruising families. Wherever we are in the world, we tend to seek out the same family-friendly anchorages, such as in the Caribbean; places where there are likely to be other cruising kids and other parents who get what it's like. Providing kids with opportunities to hang out with other cruising kids is something cruising parents crave like a drug. A friendship might only last for the half hour your child is at a playground or on a beach, or it might last for days or weeks, if two or more families decide to stay at anchor together or to follow the same route for a while, giving their kids the opportunity to play together and the parents the chance to hang out.

Cruising friendships often happen organically. You drop anchor and notice that a neighboring boat has all the tell-tale signs: tiny washing hanging out to dry, little bikes on the foredeck, a teddy bear dressed in a pink glittery tutu sitting atop the compass. Or you hear on the grapevine that there's another cruising family nearby and you seek them out over Channel 16 or set out in your tender to find them. Bart says, "We try to find children the same age and we try to see if we can stick around a little bit longer with each other. It's easy, because other parents are looking for other boats with children as well."

"We dropped anchor in Bayona, in northern Spain," Martina recalls, "next to another boat also flying a UK flag." After only a few minutes, four-year old Lily noticed that someone on the coach roof of the other boat was holding a teddy bear aloft. Lily and Katie grabbed their teddies and climbed up on their own coach roof and held up their teddies. Over the next few minutes, there was a back-and-forth toy show. "Within 20 minutes, the tender from the other boat was on its way over and the girls' mum was introducing herself. An hour later, we were all hanging out on the beach." A friendship quickly developed and, after a few days, the two families decided to sail together, only separating along the Portuguese coast when the other boat needed unexpected repairs that delayed the family's progress by some weeks.

Namia Beach, Fiji *(Mothership)*

The crew of *Mothership* went even further when they met a flotilla of US Mormon liveaboards in the Caribbean. You'll find out in Chapter 5 how that chance meeting turned into an educational travel adventure.

In some parts of the world, finding other cruising families isn't quite so easy. Jessica and Jeroen were disappointed by the lack of cruising families in the Mediterranean. Given strict education laws in some European countries, many families choose to sail for only a year or two with their pre-school children. "And most of those families tend to use that time to cross the Atlantic to the Caribbean. They don't usually go to the Mediterranean," Jessica says.

Luckily, there are now some great online resources, including our own SeaPeople app, to help you locate other cruising families and even to arrange meet-ups for your children.

Look out too for cruising family meet-ups organized by sailing/cruising associations or boat shows. They're a great way to become part of a community even before you set sail and to get advice and support from like-minded families. Kim and Bart attended one such meet-up organized by the Dutch sailing magazine *Zeilen*, for people who intended to set sail from the Netherlands in 2021. The owners of sixty boats attended, including ten families who decided to create a WhatsApp group. "When we all first set sail, we were like a little Dutch village. We used the app to say where they were and it made it easier to meet up with other families with children."

Finding cruising families online

SeaPeople

In 2024, we launched our own social networking app for cruisers. Cruising families can apply filters to locate other families with kids of similar ages in the same area. Playdates have never been so easy to organize! https://seapeopleapp.com/slv

Facebook groups

Facebook hosts a variety of private groups that are easy to join:

— Sail4Kids is a worldwide community with 7.4k members. A monthly location roll-call of where boats are and the ages of the kids on board allows everyone to see who else is currently in their cruising grounds.

— Sailing With Kids is a mostly Europe/Mediterranean/UK community of 4.3k members that allows cruising families to connect.

Liveaboard Sailing Families (with Kids) has 4.9k members. As well as sharing ideas about home schooling, family life, cooking, and socializing, this group allows you to see where other families are located and to schedule meetups.

— You can also find smaller private Facebook communities that welcome members who are cruising or planning to cruise in specific countries or parts of the world.

While Facebook pages and formal meet-ups offer great opportunities to meet children of similar ages, don't overlook the chance for your children to hang out with older or younger kids. The age-based formal education system would have us believe that children need to and should be with children of their own age. Cruising kids don't see age boundaries that way and it's not unusual to find a group of yachtie kids across a wide age range hanging out together, often with the older kids helping the younger ones out. "There was a lovely girl of nine years old," Kim recalls. "She liked to sort of play babysitting with Liz…not really babysitting…they played together. She did, of course, get bored of being with a three-year-old after a couple of days."

Local kids

Younger children are generally less self-conscious about making friends and language is often less of a barrier than it is for older children or adults. Lenny and Darwin have met local children at playgrounds or on beaches in Vietnam and Thailand and, within minutes, they've started to play together, despite not having a language in common.

Like a growing number of cruising parents, Riley and I are taking a more relaxed and blended approach to the boys' education. I'll return to this a little later on, but with regard to socializing, we have found that enrolling the boys in local kindergartens is a great way for them to socialize with local kids for a few hours each week. Lenny went to daycare in Antigua when he was two years old and pre-school in the Bahamas when he was three, and both boys have dipped in and out of various daycares when we've decided to stay in one place for a couple of weeks or more. Bart and Kim also enrolled Liz in kindergarten when they sat out hurricane season in Curaçao. "It was great for all of us," Bart admits, but especially for Liz who became friends with the local kids.

It's not uncommon for cruising families to sit out unsafe sailing seasons at anchor in more out of the way places. Our experience, and that of other families, is that kindergartens (and schools – see Chapter

5) in smaller towns and villages are generally not oversubscribed and are open to the short-term enrollment of cruising kids. Depending on where you are in the world, you might have to pay to enroll your child or you might avail of free public education services for all children, irrespective of their residency status.

When making friends is a bit more tricky

Some parents are surprised to discover that their children don't easily dive head first into quick and sudden friendships. Jessica and Jeroen were troubled when making friends proved more of a challenge for Benjamin and Frank than they had anticipated. "When we left the Netherlands, we thought that kids can play with other kids in any language," Jeroen says. They discovered, however, that the boys were shy around both local and cruising kids. Language was the primary barrier. "That was a shock," Jeroen admits. "Honestly, it worried us. We thought that we were setting them back socially, that they'd become socially awkward children." Jessica agrees: "We even considered going home." The couple decided to be patient. "It turned out that the boys just needed a little time to adjust to this new

Making friends in Fiji (*Mothership*)

life as well," Jeroen says. They started to learn a little English and, by the time they were cruising through Portugal, they were less shy around Portuguese children, who learn English from kindergarten. "It helped that they could make themselves understood even a little bit," Jessica says.

The couple admits that their boys have the best times when they meet other Dutch cruising families. "They go all out," Jessica says. "It's like a big party for them. They're best friends instantly." Jessica and Jeroen now feel much more relaxed about the boys' socialization. "Once we saw how much they enjoy being with other Dutch children, playing in their own language, the worry went away," Jeroen says. And, as the boys become increasingly proficient in English, their confidence grows in befriending native English-speaking children and others, like themselves, who use English as their lingua franca.

Family-friendly cruising grounds

Here are some of our favorite places for friendly and welcoming locals:

Indonesia: the culture is extremely family-friendly, and your kids will be adored and looked after by everyone.

Portugal: this is the PERFECT place for children. Outgoing personalities coupled with a laidback lifestyle make it easy to connect with local families. In addition, a lot of people speak English.

Mediterranean: The family-friendly cultures of Greece, Italy and the Spanish Balearic Islands makes going ashore with kids a delight.

Nurturing family relationships

Many grandparents and other loved ones struggle with the idea of their little ones being so far from home and, let's face it, cruising parents often feel guilty for creating that distance. Most babies and toddlers don't understand that the face of the person in the phone is (a) an actual live person and (b) their loved one who misses them very much. However, by the time your kids are three or four years old, they are much more interactive and communicative, and those relationships, even at a distance, can be cultivated and nurtured. With high-speed internet solutions available pretty much everywhere in the world these days, maintaining those important relationships with family and friends back home has never been easier. We've recently installed Starlink and, to quote Taj again, 'it's a game changer' (Elon, you should put that on the box). Forget about video calls that go something like this:

Grandparent:	Hey, how are you?
Grandchild:	Fine.
Grandparent:	What have you been up to?
Grandchild:	Nothing.

Within seconds, you've retrieved the device from your kid's grubby hands and are filling in the silence.

With a couple of tablets or smart phones, your kids and their loved ones back home can now enjoy much more engaging and interactive time together. Here are some of our favorite video-call ideas to inspire you:

- Read a bedtime story together – supply grandparents or other loved ones with hard or digital copies of your kids' favorite books – or send them to their local library to choose the books they want to read to their grandchildren

- Bake together – plan ahead with your loved ones back home; decide what ingredients you'll need, and be on hand to help your kids out

- Enjoy a special meal together – celebrate special occasions, or schedule a once-a-week family dinner via video call. Make it even more special by coordinating in advance so that the menu is the same in both locations

• Teach a skill – maybe your loved one back home has a skill they can teach to your child via regular video call – how to play a musical instrument, painting, knitting, Zumba, whatever it is, include your loved ones in your child's growth and development.

One important piece of advice is to always make it clear that there will be times when, owing to poor sailing conditions, boat problems, or other obstacles that often get in the way of meeting deadlines or schedules, you may not be available on a set time or day. There's nothing scarier for grandparents who lack sailing experience to not be able to make contact when they're expecting to. There will be times in your cruising life when you can easily keep your video call commitments and times when your plans will have to be more fluid. Be honest. If possible, take them sailing with you some time. Participating in cruising family life, even for only a weekend or a short vacation, should make them much more relaxed and confident about the lifestyle choices you've made.

Education and Development

Now is the time when parents, no matter what their living arrangements, start to think more about their children's education. It's also a time when, irrespective of your plans for education, you're engaging in more education-type activities with your kids.

Keep calm about education and development

Your kid is developing at a crazy pace, learning new things every day. Some parents start to worry that their kid will 'fall behind' if they're not attending kindergarten or pre-school with other kids.

Here's my advice: relax. Seriously. Your kid is not going to fall behind. Every single day of cruising life they are exposed to one hundred new learning experiences. Your kid is learning all the time – whether it's joining you on a trip to the market, helping out on and below deck, meeting people of different ages who speak different languages, playing with other kids, going to beaches, cities, forests, and everywhere else you explore as a family.

And there are also lots of great ways to sneak education in without your kid even knowing about it:

- Bake together as a way to talk about and think about numbers, weights, and measures.

- Plan your sailing route together using paper or electronic charts to help your kid become familiar with numbers, distances, navigation.

- Expand the learning potential of family excursions. If you are visiting a volcano, watch a short animation about how volcanoes work, make a clay model of a volcano, make volcano art. If you visit a museum, take some art supplies with you, find a place to sit down, and draw some items at the museum.

- Learn from the natural environment around you – dolphins, sunsets, phosphorescence, waves, wind, fish you catch, birds – these are all opportunities for conversation, for play, for experience, for thinking, talking, making art. The opportunities for learning while cruising are literally endless.

Parents sometimes worry that their children will lack opportunities to learn common childhood skills, such as riding a bike or roller skating. I think that worry comes from a misunderstanding that you will spend all your time onboard your boat. (In fact, this concern comes from the same place as the question I'm often asked about how the boys ever learned to walk.) The boat is our home, but we don't spend all of our time on it. Lenny learned to ride a bike when he was two years old and we were cruising in the Canary Islands. It was a bit of a challenge finding an even piece of road for him to learn on, but after a day of sailing we found it. We took the bike ashore in the tender each time we went, and he learned the same way other kids do. After a week of riding his bike, the novelty wore off a bit and he went back to swimming being his favorite activity.

Toys, books, digital resources

Toys: Kids like to and need to have things that are their own. It's important to make space on your boat for your child's things. Riley is scared of clutter and having too many things onboard. We have found that one large basket of toys under the saloon table is more than enough. Having it so easily accessible is great too. We always ask the boys to clean up their toys at the end of each play session. That's become part of their playtime too – throwing the rubber duckies and pieces of Lego back into the basket!

Most cruising kids are big Lego fans. It's endlessly versatile and they can get years of fun from it. "We stored our Lego in a big circular cloth bag with a drawstring all the way around," Martina says. "The bag opened out into a large circle that covered much of their forward berth. Even now, at 13 and 14 years old, they get a new Lego set each Christmas. It's become a family tradition!"

Lenny and Darwin also love magnetic tiles and fidgety toys. Jigsaw puzzles are great too, and you can often pick them up in second hand shops or from other cruising families. Playdough is always a winner. Finding a recipe online and making your own only adds to the fun.

There are, however, a couple of drawbacks to these small toys. Every parent knows what it's like to step barefoot onto a piece of Lego. That's bad enough. But what happens when a small toy gets into parts of the boat that it shouldn't? Every sailing parent has a

Lego fans *(Carina of Devon)*

story of toilets and cockpit drains blocked by small toys. "Our deck wasn't watertight and we had to regularly pump the bilge," Carola says. "Sometimes the pump would fail and when we emptied the bilge under the engine room we'd find Lego and Barbie shoes all over the floor and more blocking the bilge pump." Small toys stuck in places they shouldn't be is an occupational hazard of being a cruising parent. You come to expect it.

There simply isn't enough room for larger toys on most boats. However, Carola's children had a train set that was permanently set up and took up quite a lot of space. Lots of families, ours included, have bicycles and scooters onboard, which also take up space. Children quickly outgrow their bicycles and, as our boys grow, they upgrade to bigger bikes. If you cruise in family friendly cruising grounds, then you're likely to have opportunities to pass your outgrown bikes to other families and to be offered bigger bikes from other children who have outgrown theirs.

Books: We all want our kids to be readers, but books take up a lot of space and are heavy. Despite taking onboard what they thought were too many books, Jessica and Jeroen's sons soon knew all of them by heart. Jessica recommends library membership instead. Not only are you supporting your local library (back in your home country), but you will open up a vast and completely free online library for your kids. The Netherlands children's catalogue, which Jessica and Jeroen have access to, consists of over 9000 books and a smaller catalogue of audio books. "It's like reading proper books, except on the iPad," Jeroen says. Jessica adds, "The boys love that there's a new book pretty much every day." Most countries now have similar extensive online public library services for registered library members, so if you're not already a member, make sure to join your local library before you set sail. There are other digital reading options too. ABCmouse (see below), for example, includes an extensive online library including a wide selection of 'read aloud' books.

I have a Kindle which I read non-stop and I have downloaded lots of children's books that I can read aloud to the boys. Unlike the iPad, there are no pictures in the Kindle; however, it's a handy backup when the iPads inevitably run flat and we forget to recharge them in time for story time.

Digital resources: There are lots of great digital educational resources available. We allow Lenny and Darwin to have one or two hours on the iPad every day, mostly on educational sites. Their (and our) two favorites are Khan Academy and ABCmouse. Khan Academy is a global educational non-profit organization providing free online pre-kindergarten to Grade 12 educational resources. No matter your child's age, Khan Academy is fantastic. ABCmouse is a digital educational program specifically for early learners aged 2 to 8 years. It covers a range of early education skills, including literacy and numeracy, science and social science, music and art, which it teaches through games, puzzles, and videos. The program can be used online or offline, which is useful if you have limited or no internet coverage. It costs US$12.99 per month, which can be cancelled at any time (it often runs offers so you can access it at a reduced cost).

My advice is to find one or two digital resources that suit your child. Do some research to find out what parents and educational scholars have to say about them, to be assured of their quality or value.

Make the most of these precious years

No matter how busy we are (see Chapters 7 and 8), we make time every day to slow down and do something together as a family – to explore our local surroundings or hang out together on the boat. These days, after Darwin's nap, we often spend our afternoons outside on the trampolines, swimming off the back of the boat, snorkeling off the tender, or playing at the nearest beach. The boys love to bounce and those trampolines give them (and us) hours of fun. Before Darwin could swim, he'd sit in a big bucket on the back of *La Vagabonde II* and happily paddle in there while Lenny got in the sea for a swim. Now that they're confident swimmers, it's playtime for all four of us in the sea.

Carola says that slowing down was the key to happy liveaboard family life when her children were young. "We met sailing families who would do in six days what we did in six weeks. They wouldn't take the time to visit the countryside around the harbor, or to take their bikes out. We sometimes stayed for ten days in one place. We once went some place for Christmas and liked it so much we stayed until April. Slowing down is a good thing."

Safety

As children grow and become more independent, safety precautions evolve. It's essential that you establish non-negotiable lifejacket rules from the start so they become second nature to your kids. Every boat is different and the places where lifejackets must be worn will depend on your boat and the circumstances. In a production-built monohull, for instance, your rule might be that your kids always wear a lifejacket when above deck. But you might have conditions to this rule. Jessica and Jeroen's waiver to this rule, for instance, is that the boys can be in the cockpit without their life jackets *if* sea conditions are calm *and* both parents are in the cockpit too. "But, when there's any kind of sea state or if there are dolphins or anything to cause excitement, then they need to have the lifejackets on," Jeroen says. Martina and Julian's girls could be in the cockpit without life jackets, but tethered. However, if you have a bigger boat, such as Hazel and Dave's refurbished fishing trawler, then your lifejacket rules may be more relaxed.

Where your children can be, with or without a lifejacket, will also depend on circumstances. Jeroen and Jessica's boys are not allowed out of the cockpit while at sea, except to see dolphins and only then if both parents are with them on the foredeck. Martina

Benjamin and Frank in their lifejackets *(Sans Souci)*

and Julian's girls had to be tethered to the jackstay running along the deck if they left the cockpit.

With children moving around the deck with increasing independence, many families put netting around the sides. While many put it all around their boat, Jeroen and Jessica decided to only place it from aft to the midship gates, port and starboard. "They're not allowed out of the cockpit when we're at sea anyway," Jeroen says, "so they would never be forward of those gates without us holding on to them."

Martina suggests that the netting around *Carina of Devon* had more of a psychological than practical effect. "When the girls got older, we took the netting off. At first, it felt more dangerous, because the netting wasn't there. But the only effect was that I lost more clothes pegs, small tools, and things like that overboard."

Familiarize yourself with the danger points around your boat from the perspective of your kids. Determine what alterations you need to make and what rules you need to have in place regarding access to those danger points.

Liz and the safety net *(Tranquillity)*

Tips:

- Engage with the cruising community: get out there and meet other sailors and other cruising families. Your entire family will benefit from the experience.

- Create opportunities for your kids to meet and play with local kids in parks, playgrounds, play groups, or events.

- Don't stress about education: your kids are learning so much every day, their minds expanding with new experiences. They'll be absolutely fine!

- Establish safety rules based on the danger points on your boat and the needs of your family.

Chapter 5

Primary to pre-teens

"In the Bocas del Torro islands in Panama, we would do errands with my mum. At the end of the day, we'd be hungry, hot, and tired, and we'd go to a stall where a woman sold us fried chicken. We got to know the woman. It was really nice. I remember sitting down, eating chicken, relaxing, looking at the sunset, and then going back to the boat."

That's Yewan. He's eleven and has been circumnavigating the globe with his brother, sister, and parents since he was eight. He and his siblings have countless tales to tell – hand-feeding nursing sharks from a beach on a Pacific island; seeing sloths, fire ants, and water snakes almost daily in Suriname; busking on streets from Greece to New Zealand; hiking volcanos from the Mediterranean to the South Pacific; spearfishing, dinghy sailing, and kayaking; befriending cruising kids of different ages, cultures, backgrounds, and nationalities, and finding ingenious ways to maintain those friendships. But, of all his incredible adventures, it was the simple act of eating fried chicken, befriending the woman who cooked it, and enjoying the sunset that Yewan recalled as his fondest memory of the past two years.

My boys are still a bit young and we've only recently started to actively home school Lenny. But I've learned a lot from other parents and have lots of great ideas for the next few years with my own kids. Education and socializing are the two preoccupations of parents when their kids are in the primary-school age years, so that's the focus of this chapter. You'll find some great ideas for younger kids here too, but the focus is mainly on 6–7-year-olds up to pre- and early teens.

Prepping for cruising life

If you've been cruising since your kids were little then it's normal life for them. But if you're setting sail for the first time, it's important that you support your kids as they transition to this new lifestyle. Some children will be very excited, while others may struggle with leaving behind friends, school, family members, or home. Some may resist altogether. Most children will be torn between wanting to leave and wanting to stay. It is important that you include your children in all stages of planning and preparation, and that you listen to, discuss, and explore ways to help them overcome their fears and concerns.

Taj and Bella were 10 and 8 years old when they set sail from New South Wales aboard *Catalpa*. "They were forming deeper friendships," says Sara, "having sleepovers, wanting to hang out with their friends all the time." Sara and Lee had instilled their long-term dream of becoming cruisers since the children were young, but it took some years to set the dream in motion. Sara believes that waiting even one more year might have made all the difference, given the friendships they were forming. Initially, they sailed for weeks at a time, returning to school between trips[8]. Taj has fond memories of the gradual transition they made onto the boat: "We lived on land, but we'd pack a bag and hop on the boat." Later, they gradually moved onto the boat, while still attending school. "We were still in school until a couple of weeks before we left for good."

---

8   The family was supported by very understanding teachers, whose only advice was that the children keep journals to record their experiences.

Giving your kids a sense of shared ownership of both the sailing plan and of the boat, and being sensitive to their fears and concerns will certainly make for a smoother transition. Consider too their spaces on the boat, give them the freedom (ensuring safety and practicality) to take ownership of their onboard spaces, and be empathetic to their need to surround themselves with familiar toys, games, books, and objects.

Education

Irenka has successfully educated three children while circumnavigating the globe. She says, "On top of boat maintenance, schooling is the most challenging thing you're going to do." We're up for that challenge, right? Like every other aspect of cruising life with kids, the trick to success is to take it slowly, establish a routine, and embrace it as part of your everyday life. "When you have kids aboard," Irenka says, "schooling has to happen before anything else. It takes time and often your plans have to evolve around having that [school] time each morning." Here, I share some common education concerns, provide an overview to different approaches to educating while cruising, and troubleshoot common problems.

Common concerns

I'm not a teacher

"The thing that scared me most about cruising was the idea of home schooling," says Sara. "I didn't worry about sailing around the world, about the weather, the ocean, none of that. The scariest thing for me was that I'd be in charge of the kids' education. I'm not a bookish person. I was terrified." Sara's concerns are not uncommon. Most parents worry they won't be up to the task, that they won't know how to structure the *school* day, that they won't know enough to *teach* their children, and that they won't know how to *assess* their kids' progress.

Education on board
(Above: Carina of Devon)
(Below: Argo)

You shouldn't be scared. First, the joy of home education is that it's not school. Even if you follow a formal curriculum, the time and space you devote to education can be flexible and suited to your lifestyle. Second, instead of *teaching* your children, think of your role as (a) facilitating their learning, i.e., putting in place the conditions that allow them to learn, and (b) learning with them. I don't mean just admitting that you don't know something and then learning it together with your children. I mean going on a learning adventure with your children and learning together about the world you live in.

My children will fall behind

When they set out on their open-ended circumnavigation, Irenka worried that her children would fall behind their peers: "You hold the burden of responsibility and you don't know what will happen if they don't learn." However, this concern was entirely unfounded. When Rowan left *Mothership* in Tahiti and returned to the UK, aged 16, to continue her education, she found herself top of the class in English and Maths and equal to her peers in other subjects. She also discovered she had a more mature approach to learning than many of her peers.

When Katie and Reuben returned to formal education in the UK, they found that, although they hadn't fallen behind, they had, in some areas, covered different material to their peers. Reuben's classmates, for example, had learned to do joined up writing, but he had not. "He caught up quickly," Hazel says. "Both kids did."

Many cruising kids return to formal education to find that they are more self-motivated than their peers, having developed self-learning skills during their months or years of cruising. As Irenka says of Rowan, "She was pretty much self-taught the last year she was on the boat."

Develop good practices

Putting a few simple practices in place will ensure that your kids' education runs (relatively) smoothly and will be a learning experience for the entire family:

- Accept that education will take up at least a couple of hours of your time each day

- Be honest with yourself when things aren't working and be willing to keep changing and reinventing your approach

- Give yourself a break – remind yourself that you are doing a great job

- Enjoy the unconventionality of it all

Apart from these general rules to live by, here are some common practices that will set you up for home schooling success.

Prepare in advance

Before setting sail, or before your kids reach an age where you have to seriously think about their education, consider what education looks like to you. Research different pedagogies (see below). You might be surprised by how many different approaches there are. Think about what will work for your family. Do you want to focus on one specific approach? Or create a hybrid of multiple approaches? Remember, there is no one correct way to educate your children. Remain open to change and adapt as you go.

Taj and Bella's teachers suggested two options – continue to be enrolled in school as distance learners or be home schooled. "We didn't know there were so many other options," Sara admits. Potential limited internet access while cruising meant that distance learning was not an option. Sara and Lee also didn't want their kids to feel under pressure to complete and submit assignments to a strict schedule. "That would take away from the purpose of what we wanted to do," Sara says. Instead, they decided to home educate.

Routine

At the risk of sounding like a broken record, establishing an education routine will benefit everyone on board. Keep it short. Most cruising kids spend no more than a couple of hours each day engaged in core educational activities – reading, writing, maths, science, social science. Any more than that and everyone quickly burns out and you'll have mutiny on your hands. Early morning, directly after breakfast, is a common time for semi-formal or formal learning. "If they start playing before we do school, we lose them," says Jeroen of his sons, who follow a formal Dutch curriculum. A post-breakfast education routine leaves most of the day free for the rest of cruising life.

Find a routine that works, and stick to it. If it's not working, change it. Periodically review your routine to see if it needs tweaking or even a complete overhaul. Aboard *Mothership*, Monday to Thursday mornings are for maths, reading, and writing, with science, social science, music, art, or other subjects covered once or twice each week. Every Friday is Boat Day, when the children learn about navigation, meteorology, rope work, engine maintenance, or focus on the oceanography or marine biology around them.

Creating an education routine, and sticking to it, will make learning a habit. But remember, routines are sometimes made to be broken, and when a great opportunity presents itself, put your routine on the shelf for the day and go have fun! Why else are you here?

Educate on passage

Watch routines, changes to sleeping patterns, weather, waves, and leaning vessels all pose a challenge to home education routines. "I know families that home school on passage," Irenka says. She regrets that her family didn't establish that routine from the outset, as she often feels under pressure to 'catch up' on home schooling 'lost' while *Mothership* has been on a long passage. The children now associate passage making with home school-free time and changing that mindset has been far from easy. Irenka's advice? From your very first passage, practice educating while the boat is moving. Moving aboard *La Vagabonde III* has coincided with Lenny beginning home schooling. We've already embraced this wisdom and, whether at anchor or under way, Lenny now spends a little time a few days each week working on his literacy and numeracy.

Education on passage won't be the same as education at anchor. Discuss with each other and with your kids what your expectations are, when routine education time is likely to occur, which parent (or other adult crew member) will be responsible, and whether a greater level of educational independence will be expected of your children while under way.

Don't treat it like school

This piece of advice is perhaps the most freeing but also the hardest to grasp. Most of us have only known formal education and find it hard to get our heads around a more relaxed approach to learning. But here goes: Rid yourself of the mindset that home education will be the same as school. "You've got to be dynamic and really flexible," Woody says. "You want to give your kids as much experience as possible and let them put the bits together. Trying to be structured, like in school, is too restrictive." When the family first set sail, they tried to emulate the school environment. "It brought a lot of stress onto the boat, for us and the kids," he says. "After a while we loosened up." This means shorter duration, being flexible about where your kids study (saloon table might be the best place, but is it the only place?), and their study resources.

Manage your expectations

A common home-schooling mistake is trying to pack too much in. "I used to have big ideas," Hazel recalls. "We'll do this, then this, then this. When we only got through one thing, I'd feel frustrated. We never did as much in our allocated hours as I hoped." Hazel's expectations for what could be achieved, for her children's concentration levels, and for her own patience, were too high. Start off small. Focus on only one or two subjects in each session. If you get through those, give yourself and your kids a pat on the back. And don't beat yourself up if you don't. Some activities, such as learning to read or learning a new maths concept, are extremely tiring on kids and can only be done in short bursts.

Go with the flow

Self-imposed pressure to catch up, to keep up with some imagined ideal, can suck the joy out of sailing. What's the point? Better to trust that your kids are learning just by being in the world. Cover the basics of literacy and numeracy and trust your kids to learn. "We're supposed to be catching up in New Zealand," Irenka says. "But we're doing a lot of moving around and then interesting things are going on that we don't want to miss and we forget to do schooling." The joy of home schooling is that you can postpone it when you like, to do more fun things with your kids.

Now that the crew of *Ros Ailithir* has moved ashore, Hazel misses the freedom and adaptability of home education. "The children were much more active than they are now. They'd join us in whatever we were doing. We'd do school in the morning and then go out and explore in the afternoons. I miss the freedom we used to have."

Be open to learning opportunities

The crew of *Mothership* are my heroes. Their self-devised curriculum never gets in the way of unexpected opportunities to learn. When a fellow cruiser in Greece offered to give Darry violin lessons, and when they found another violin teacher in Spain, they put the curriculum aside so he could focus on those brief opportunities to improve his violin skills. When they realized how inexpensive it would be to go skiing in Greece, they jumped at the chance for the children to learn to ski. When an artist, who follows the family on Instagram, offered private art lessons, they began sporadic Zoom classes designed specifically for their kids. And, while cruising in the Caribbean, they met and befriended a flotilla of Mormon families, including 22 children of all ages, with whom they cruised for three months. The three children from *Mothership* learned alongside their new friends. "All the kids did a marine biology class together twice a week," Irenka says. "We all took turns to teach it. It was brilliant."

The family also participates in a GOES Foundation[9] citizen science project. Using a kit provided by the foundation, they collect water samples which they photograph under a microscope, and send to the GOES lab for analysis. "It's fun," Darry says. "We scoop up water in the middle of the ocean, put in on the microscope, and try to identify what we see – is it plastic, or small algae, microbes." The foundation then shares the research results with the citizen scientists.

Let the *Mothership* crew be a lesson to us all: stay open to opportunities to learn from or with other cruisers, and from unexpected encounters along the way.

Approaches to education

Cruising families, whether they are aware of it or not, generally have developed a hybrid education for their kids, drawn from multiple approaches.

Formal curriculum

You might choose, or be required, to follow the curriculum set by your school, state, or home country, or a curriculum set by an international

---

9   https://goesfoundation.com/

organization or online learning resource. The advantages of a formal curriculum may include:

- A course of study to follow (textbooks, online resources, etc.), often with teaching guidelines

- Formal classes, tutorials, or other interactive learning with professional educators

- Guidelines for how much work should be covered per day/week

- Scheduled assignments and/or exams

- Metrics to measure your child's progress

However, there are also disadvantages to this type of curriculum, including:

- Lack of flexibility

- Need for internet access to participate in time-specific online activities and to submit assignments

- Need to submit evidence that your child is meeting curriculum targets

- You might be required to carry a lot of textbooks and workbooks on board

"We've met families whose children follow an educational curriculum online and who have to submit regular assignments and take exams," Sara says. "That would be overwhelming for me. I don't want my kids to be anxious and nervous about learning. For the people who choose to do that, it's still a beautiful way to live. But that type of schooling isn't for us."

Devise your own curriculum

Creating a curriculum that suits your circumstances and your children's needs is a more workable option for many. This might be loosely based on or be a mash-up of formal curricula, together with aspects of the curriculum of your own design. For instance, you might use a language app to learn a new language, delve into BBC Bite Size, Khan Academy, or other similar resources to take a specific course of study, or sign up for a MOOC (massive open online course). A home-made curriculum is one in which you decide when, what, and how to educate your children, providing them with a focus of study and the resources to achieve specific targets. It offers the freedom of take advantage of learning opportunities as they arise and allows learning to be guided by your child's interests.

There are certain advantages to creating your own curriculum, including:

- It is a bespoke curriculum designed to the specific needs and interests of your child

- The curriculum can evolve, expand, and contract as the need arises

- The design can reflect the digital and technological abilities of your boat and can include a broad range of online, offline, paper, and other resources

- You and your child can work at your own pace

- There is no pressure to meet pre-determined achievement metrics

However, the disadvantages to a home-made curriculum include:

- Lack of metrics for comparison to peers

- Often a lack of resources to support the parent/ teacher

- In the absence of external motivators (assignment deadlines, exam dates), it may be difficult to stay on task or to reach self-imposed targets

Learning by doing

This approach to education focuses on learning through experience and practice. Opportunities to learn present themselves in the everyday lives of cruising children. Sara says, "We pull into a new dock and everyone's speaking at us in another language and we've got to go source our food and go to the emigration office and check into the country. Then the kids will play with some kid who doesn't speak their language." Such regular activities provide children with valuable life skills for dealing with novel situations, in novel places, often in languages they cannot yet speak.

Cruising offers opportunities for the entire family to learn by doing. If you are open to the possibilities offered by the situations you find yourself in, then you and your children can learn together.

For the crew of *Mothership*, an opportunity to climb the active Mt Vesuvius in Italy, followed by a visit to Herculaneum, a town destroyed by the volcano in AD 79, has led to an ongoing fascination with volcanoes. "You couldn't get a better lesson on volcanos than that," Woody says. The family has continued to hike volcanos and visit volcano museums in countries all along their circumnavigation route and volcanos have inspired onboard lessons in volcanology, geography, history, culture, and economics. The family uses online and onboard resources, and devises lessons to suit the children's ages and abilities. "Once we've stimulated their interest in a particular subject," Woody says, "we might watch a documentary about it. After that, they might go off and do their own research or projects, based on what interests them. Darry, for instance, loves animation, so he might make an animation about volcanoes or earthquakes." Friday Boat Day aboard *Mothership* is the quintessential learning by doing day. The children learn about useful boat knowledge, such as knots, radar, first aid, and also study subjects relevant to sailing, such as meteorology, by learning about the current weather, or marine biology, by diving on a reef, observing fish behavior, or dissecting a recently speared fish.

The advantages to this approach to learning include:

- It is flexible and adaptable to interests and opportunities as they arise

- Knowledge and skills are learned holistically (mind and body)

- Learning together as a family

- It allows you to make use of available resources in the world around you and online.

However, as with devising your own curriculum, learning by doing doesn't offer metrics to compare your children with their peers and, in the absence of external motivators and such a variety of learning opportunities to choose from, having a focus may be difficult.

Home schooling and the law

The right to home educate children varies from country to country. For example, home education in permitted in Australia and in all 50 US states, although the regulations vary in strictness between states. Meanwhile, at the other extreme, in the Netherlands, France, and Germany, home education is so limited that it almost does not exist at all. Opting to exclude children from the education system may exclude parents from tax obligations and pension rights, and can incur fines. One option for families from countries with stricter education laws is to formally emigrate to another country. Some families, cruising for shorter time periods (1–2 years), and with supportive teachers, play the system by paying for GP's certificates that excuse their children from school.

No matter what country you come from, it is important that you understand and, where necessary, follow the educational guidelines; otherwise, you may face matriculation and social security challenges down the line.

Unschooling

Unschooling is a radical approach to education that trusts children to follow their own interests, and to learn what they need to know when they need to know it. The role of the parent is to facilitate the child's learning, providing them with resources and opportunities, and assisting the child to learn when they ask for help. You know when a kid falls in love with something (dinosaurs, a sports team, Marvel movies) and then finds out everything they can about that subject? That's unschooling, except that it applies to everything your kid learns.

One aspect of this approach is that you give your kid the freedom to delve as deeply into a subject as they want. So, if your kid wants to learn only about Norse gods to the exclusion of everything else (maths, language, history, music, etc.), then you leave them to it. The theory is that when they've exhausted that subject and are ready to move on to something else, they will. (In Chapter 6, you'll meet some teenagers who've transitioned to unschooling).

Yewan developed an interest in playing music by going busking with his older brother and sister. Too young at first to play, he held out the hat for tips, while his siblings played. He then taught himself to play the ukelele and guitar from instructional YouTube videos. Now he busks with his brother. They practice their half-hour set of five songs, played on guitar and ukelele, and improvise and experiment with other instruments. Each new place they visit, they figure out the most opportune times and locations for busking. Yewan is currently saving up his share of their earnings to buy a new ukelele. Left to their own devices, the siblings have learned, among other things, music, finances, planning, teamwork, and marketing.

Left alone too, Darry taught Yewan how to spearfish; together, they have learned to gut, cook, and serve fish, to light and tend a fire, and to cook over a fire. Darry, meanwhile, has taught himself how to make wildlife animations which he posts on his own YouTube

Opportunities for learning *(Mothership)*

channel and has developed his interest in ecology by keeping an ant colony aboard *Mothership*.

Unschooling is not for the faint-hearted. It takes a certain level of confidence in your kid's innate ability to want and have the capacity to learn about the world around them. Parents who choose unschooling as their dominant form of education are not interested in comparing their kids to peers, or against standardized metrics of learning and development. (see Resources for two books on the theory and practice of unschooling).

Formal education

If you're new to cruising, you might be surprised to learn that some cruising kids go to bricks and mortar schools. How, you might ask. Well, cruising isn't all about being on the high seas all the time and there are many reasons for dropping anchor in one location for a few months – boat repairs, paid employment, discovering a place you love, or simply wanting to take a break from constant planning, weather watching, and being on the move.

"We dropped anchor in little piece of paradise in Spain," Martina says, "next to a family with three boys, all of whom were temporarily enrolled in the village school. We never planned to send our kids to school, but the chance for them to learn Spanish and to be immersed in Spanish culture for a term or two, in a tiny three-teacher school, was too good to pass up." Martina and Julian weren't the first cruisers to have this idea and, pre-COVID, the little three-teacher school had a steady stream of cruising kids enrolling for a month, a term, or a school year. Indeed, Hazel's and Martina's kids became friends when they were in the same class for a term, when both families overwintered on the same stretch of river.[10]

Carola and Teddy, restricted by the Netherlands' formal education laws, enrolled their kids in school full-time in Amsterdam. Each Friday evening, the boat engine was already running when the children came home from school, ready to head out onto Ijsselmere for the weekend. During vacation time, they sailed farther afield, cruising in English, Danish, and German waters. "At every opportunity, we were gone," Carola says.

Enrolling your children in formal education

• Offers an immersive cultural experience for children and parents

• Can give parents some much-needed space in the day to work on the boat or in paid employment (perhaps while preparing for a future voyage)

• Comes with formal resources, metrics, and structure.

---

10   Sanlúcar de Guadiana on the Rio Guadiana on the southern border between Spain and Portugal.

However, the disadvantages of formal education include:

- Bureaucratic hurdles, depending on the country or region

- A short period of time may not be enough for your kid to settle into a new school (especially in a different language)

- You may struggle to help your children with homework in a different language.

Hybrid education

The reality is that most cruising children enjoy a hybrid education made up of some or all these styles, and education is often made up as they go along. Sara says a weight was lifted off her shoulders when she realized she didn't have to answer to any educational authority. "It had felt like I was doing what was expected. But then, I thought, 'Sara, these are your kids, you can teach them what you want. You can handle this whatever way you want.'" This has meant reining in her own creativity and interests, and giving her kids the space to learn what and how suits them. As well as following their own creative interests (see Chapter 6), Taj and Bella have learned to speak new languages along the way, and they have a passion for reading.

Katie and Reuben's hybrid education combined formal education with learning by doing and unschooling. During extended periods moored on the south coast of England, they went by dinghy to school every day. They tried to follow the school curriculum when they went cruising, with resources from their teachers. "I looked at the curriculum online," Hazel says, "and developed teaching ideas from that." In addition, they kept daily journals, in which they recorded their travels in words and drawings, learned about the world around them by exploring and participating in it, and attended a village school in rural Spain for a term.

Learning at sea
(Above: *Ros Ailither)*
(Below: *Argo*)

Challenges

Cruising kids live amazingly varied and enriched lives, with opportunities to learn that most kids or parents can't even imagine. But education comes with certain challenges. Here are the most common ones that the other cruising families report:

My kids are unenthusiastic, rebellious, or otherwise refuse to be taught

If you think that home schooling is going to be easy and that your children will be delighted and willing vessels into which you can pour all your knowledge about the world, think again. Irenka says that most days, especially when the kids were younger, they simply didn't want to sit down for their routine learning time. "They hated it. We'd spend hours doing something that should only take a few minutes. They wouldn't concentrate. Or we'd fight with them because they refused to do it." Sara had the same experience: "We gave them motivational speeches. We bribed them with cake. You think your family is the only one like that. But then you meet other homeschooling families and you realize the exact same thing is going on."

Your kid might get glowing reports from their teachers, but you see a whole different side to them. What they're willing to do for their teacher, they refuse to do for you. They'll try every trick in the book to avoid doing school work. They're masters at it.

Experienced cruising parents have some tried and tested tricks up their sleeves (that don't necessarily involve cake).

- Novelty: For younger children, in particular, novelty pays off. Martina says, "Julian brought all the teddy bears out and they became 'students' in the saloon 'classroom'. Lily and Katie loved the teddy bears being told off for not doing their work." Also consider novel places off the boat to do school work, or the use of novel materials.

- Reward charts: Darry and Yewan receive bonus pocket money when they complete their study and chores reward charts. "But we know it won't last forever," Irenka says. "They'll be really excited about a new reward system for a few months, but the excitement wears off and we have to think of something else."

- Take turns educating: When possible, share and swap educating roles, so that your child isn't always working exclusively with one parent. This will prevent both parent and children from getting tired or frustrated and will bring different perspectives to your child's learning.

- Consider your kid's age: Children often become more motivated as they get older and develop their own internal incentives for studying. Yewan, who's 11, shows a level of maturity and self-awareness when he says, "I don't really like schooling. I could be doing things like snorkeling or running around or going to the park. I used to think that living on the boat was like a holiday. Now I think, 'Just get it over with and then I can go out and play.'"

- Consider your kid's stage of development: A child who isn't yet a confident reader will find all subjects that require reading difficult. Irenka says, "As Yewan's reading abilities have improved, he has increasingly started to learn independently in all subjects."

Your kid's motivation will fluctuate. Sometimes they don't want to do routine education at all and other times they'll be up and have it done before you get out of bed. Try to relax about it, and trust yourself and your kids.

Home educating children of different ages

Many families include children of different ages and stages of development. Juliana and Valentin's four boys, for example, range in age from 6 to 15 years. Juggling the needs of multiple children, all using different educational resources, at different stages of learning, can be difficult, particularly if you are following formal curricula. When the children were younger, Woody and Irenka found routine education time time-consuming, as it required both to be present, one working with Rowan and the other working with Darry and Yewan. At times, it was also easier to separate the children into their own spaces. "Sometimes, the boys couldn't be in the same place, because they would fight. We had to separate them to get anything done," Woody says.

Children of different ages can at times study together, such as the *Mothership* kids learning about volcanos, but with each working to their own aptitudes and developmental stages. It's important to remember, as Woody points out, that "you're not only dealing with differences in academic ability because of their ages, but also differences in ability to concentrate and different personalities."

Children, even siblings, are not uniform in reaching developmental milestones. Avoid comparing your children. While one might learn to read at 3 years, another might not learn until they're 9. While one might excel at maths or geography, their sibling may not. They're individuals, each with unique learning styles and interests.

Educational resources

With a mix of digital and other resources, you will be prepared for education wherever you are. If you expect to have limited internet access, prepare in advance by stocking up on (a) hard copies of textbooks and other books and (b) downloadable resources.

Online educational resources

Khan Academy (https://www.khanacademy.org/) offers fantastic educational resources for children of all ages in a broad range of subject areas.

BBC Bite Size (https://www.bbc.co.uk/bitesize) includes videos and tests, and follows all levels of the UK curriculum and beyond in a vast ranges of subjects useful to students from any country.

IXL (https://uk.ixl.com/) is an international members-only site that provides personalized K–12 learning in maths and English, including following the national curricula of many countries and providing exam preparation.

Digital textbooks can be downloaded for free for kindergarten to grade 12 (and beyond). The sites are easy to use and navigate. Each comes with different functions, e.g., personal tutor, learning community, and curriculum-building options. We recommend:

CK-12 https://www.ck12.org

Open Stax https://openstax.org/k12

Core Knowledge Foundation https://www.coreknowledge.org

Books/E-readers

These days, there's no need to stock an onboard library. "We took so many books with us," Sara says, but Taj and Bella soon outgrew or read most of them. They culled their library, gave books to other families, and invested in Kindles.

E-readers or tablets are an indispensable resource with advantages over traditional books. Apart from saving on precious boat space, a vast number of books, in the languages of your choice, can be downloaded and read anywhere. The backlighting on Kindles means you can even read on night watch, and they have long battery lives and can be recharged efficiently. "They're super practical," Valentin says of the four e-readers his sons have on board. Like many cruising kids, Valentin's boys while away the hours on long passages reading from the libraries of books they've downloaded.

Learning offline

More and more cruisers are investing in Starlink technology. However, for those who don't, there will be periods of time – passage making or cruising in more remote places – when online educational resources are inaccessible. Before leaving the UK, Woody and Irenka contacted the country's biggest textbook companies and explained their plan to home educate three children while sailing around the world. The companies donated textbooks and workbooks appropriate to the children's ages at the time. The books were passed from Rowan, to Darry, and now to Yewan. While the two older siblings wrote in notebooks, Yewen gets to write directly into the workbooks. "When he's finished with them, we'll throw them away," Irenka says.

Kiwix, a downloadable encyclopedia, similar to Wikipedia, is a useful resource when you're offline. While it lacks the amount of content of an online site, the *Catalpa* crew have it found useful for researching home school projects, and for seeking answers to questions that arise in the world around them.

Friends and fun

Kids just want to have fun, right? Rest assured cruising kids don't spend all their time with their parents. They want to hang out, go exploring, make and build and create stuff, and be on the go with other kids. They want to play together with their toys, share their hobbies, do sports, play boardgames. Sure, there will be times when it's just your family unit. And those times are really great. But cruising families form a vast, fluid community who seek each other out and who seek out opportunities for their kids to meet up and play. In this 6–12 age group, kids are gaining independence and have the mental capacity and the tech skills to maintain and develop friendships over longer periods of time.

Supporting your kid's need for friends

Irenka says that three things determine where, when, and how *Mothership* sails: the weather, other kids, and the places the family wants to visit. In that order. "The weather obviously comes first," she says. "After that, we find other family boats to hang out with. Sometimes, we decide that we want to stick together for a while." This friendship-centered approach has led to the family doing different legs of their Pacific crossing in the company of other family yachts and spending three months in the Caribbean with a flotilla of families.

The ease of finding other families depends on where you are in the world. Sailing families with kids in mid- to late-childhood aren't too common in the Mediterranean, while the Caribbean is awash with family cruisers, including many from the US. However, even in the Mediterranean, there are pockets of cruising families scattered here and there. "It seems to be feast or famine in the Mediterranean when it comes to family boats," Woody says. "There are no families, and then suddenly, five or six turn up at once."

When they overwintered in Greece, Rowan, Darry, and Yewan only briefly met one other sailing family. The following year, in Almerimar, in southeast Spain, they befriended kids from three other boats and ended up spending the pandemic lockdown together. A few miles along the coast from Almerimar, Lily and Katie met no other cruising kids at their overwintering marina but, the following winter, in the Rio Guadiana, they befriended and attended school with kids from three other boats. "A whole gang of us happened to be overwintering," Martina says. "Hazel would invite my girls over to make cookies aboard *Ros Ailither*, or a whole gang of us, with kids all around the same age, would head off for a hike and to cook lunch over an open fire." The kids all hung out together, on each other's boats, or on mini-adventures ashore.

Often, families find each other organically. I shared online resources in Chapter 4 to help you find and make plans with other families cruising in your area. The important thing to remember is that every family boat is looking out for other family boats. Even if your kids aren't the same age, they'll generally be keen to play with each other. But it might mean you have to step out of your comfort zone a little. "When we see another kid's boat, we immediately make contact," Irenka says. "You do things you wouldn't normally do. 'Hello. Do you want to go and play?' You immediately start networking, swapping WhatsApps, telling each other what you are going to do today, seeing who wants to come along."

Like *Mothership* crossing the Pacific, families often buddy boat so their children can spend more time together. "After all the years we've been sailing," Woody says, "we've got quite a good network of friends who put us in contact with other people. It's very rare that we don't buddy boat up with someone." Buddying means that kids can hang out with each other in each new anchorage and on longer passages, when conditions are safe, can even visit each other's boats.

Friendships can sometimes be found in unexpected places. If those friendships are meaningful, ask yourself if you want to alter your sailing plans to spend more time with your new friends. In Curaçao, *Mothership* met and befriended a flotilla of boats from the US. "There were 22 kids in the group, aged from 6 to 17," Woody says. "They were so warm and friendly," Irenka recalls. "Such a lovely group of people." Although Mothership was headed to Bonaire, they changed their plans, joined the flotilla, and sailed for Colombia.

"We didn't know a lot about Mormons at the time," Woody says. "We had a bit of an awkward moment when they invited us to meet on the beach and we turned up with our beers, not realizing that they didn't drink." Despite these cultural differences, they hung out together for three months, sharing home education duties and undertaking a seven hours per day, four-day hike through the Colombian jungle, wading through rivers, to get to Ciudad Perdida. "They were an amazing group to do it with. It was really great for our kids," Woody says. "Those few months were a real highlight for us. There were enough kids that everyone had more than one kid their own age."

Cruising as a family means that it must work for all members of your family. Most kids at this stage of their lives just want to make friends and have fun. Therefore, your cruising plans must be adaptable and open to friendships made along the way.

Freedom to play

People are sometimes surprised by the freedom and independence cruising kids have, compared to their landlubber peers. Cruising families spend a lot of time together in different situations and parents get to observe their kids interact with a range of other people, handle themselves in different social situations, and use equipment such as outboard motors, sailing dinghies, and surfboards. By the mid-childhood years, many cruising kids are capable of simple trips to the grocery store or market in a second language, getting from boat to shore by themselves, and even foraging, spearfishing, and cooking a meal on a camp fire! By being around their kids so much, parents have a good sense of what they are capable of and, therefore, often trust them in situations that non-live aboard parents might find surprising. (I'll return to the question of personal safety in Chapter 6).

Although Sara and Lee were wary of letting Bella and Taj be alone ashore when they were younger, the two had a lot of freedom on and near the water right from the start. "They'd go off on the dinghy together," Sara says. They were often gone for hours with other sailing kids, exploring the coastline or hanging out on a nearby beach. Cruising kids often spend a lot of time in the water together, paddle boarding, kayaking, snorkeling, and spearfishing. Shorelines offer endless opportunities for kids to play and hang out, and to let their imaginations run wild.

Living in the close confines of a boat doesn't mean that play dates at home are out of the question. Timmy and Ellen's friends regularly came to play on *Maes*, with Timmy's makeshift bedroom converted, at different times, into a disco space, a cinema, and a space for Hallowe'en parties. Lily and Katie sometimes had friends for sleepovers, once having three friends at once. "They slept in our cabin, because it was the biggest space. We moved into their V-berth. Five girls, aged 7 to 10 years. They were so noisy!"

Friendship challenges

One of the challenges of cruising friendships is that you can't pick and choose who your friends are. However, Rowan believes that this experience has been to her advantage and she's much more open to being friends with kids who are different to her that she might not otherwise, on first impressions, choose to befriend. Irenka says, "We've met some great kids that our kids get on really well with, but there's often that initial transition. You might not be friends with someone straight away. But the kids have learned that even though their first impression might be 'they won't be my friend,' they have to make the effort because they don't have any other choice. Then they find out they have something in common and they get on with it."

Language can also be a challenge to friendships. However, after some initial hesitancy, kids usually find a way. Sometimes the way in is by playing with toys that have a shared cultural meaning, but don't require words – Matchbox cars, Barbies, Lego. "After a while," Darry says, "You just play with each other. Play tag. Go spear fishing. And you connect with them without language." And he should know. Yewan told me that he and his brother have made friends with cruising kids from Israel, Russia, Germany, Spain, the Netherlands, and France. In some cases, they shared little or nothing by way of a common language.

Saying goodbye

Perhaps the two biggest challenges for kids in this age range are (a) not having a constant friend or set of friends and (b) constantly saying goodbye. "Saying goodbye to new friends all the time is hard," Sara says. "It teaches you resilience though." Both Yewan and Rowan say that, at first, they used to get upset every time they parted ways with cruising friends. "At first, I was sobbing, crying," Yewan says. "I still feel sad, but now I've gotten used to it." Having developed intense friendships over the course of days or weeks, children often say goodbye expecting to not see their friends again. However, communication technology, and the ability of kids in mid-childhood to use that technology, means that, increasingly, those friendships can be maintained at a distance.

By the mid-childhood years, most kids outshine their parents when it comes to digital technology. And while we might bemoan our kids' overuse of their devices, the truth is, they allow cruising kids to maintain friendships along the way.

Darry keeps in touch with some of the friends he has made over the years, including a friend he made in Spain who now lives in Germany, and another in England. "Some friends I've kept in touch with for three years now," he says. "We play online games together and chat on Instagram." Yewen, who is younger, does not have any social media accounts. However, he has the Stars Messenger Kid Safe Chat[11] app on his phone that allows him to stay in contact with friends. Both he and Darry have also started to use the Discord app to create group chats with other cruising friends. "I've had so many friends now," Yewen says. "Hundreds and hundreds and hundreds. I meet them and then leave them. I stay in touch with some."

"Keeping in touch online is good," Irenka says, "but they really need to physically have other kids." Face-to-face friendships

---

11   For a review of other child-friendly communication apps, see this review: https://talkingparents.com/blog/apps-for-kids-to-communicate-with-family

among cruisers of all ages are, by the nature of the lifestyle, short-lived. However, cruising kids are generally much more open than their land-based counterparts to developing friendships with other children of different ages, genders, languages, and cultures.

Keeping busy

Won't my kids be bored on long passages, you might ask. Only if you treat them as passengers and not crew. Managing boredom on longer passages can be a challenge for everyone but maybe particularly for kids, if there are no other kids (or only their siblings) around.

The kids who've contributed to this book generally spend their free time on board reading, drawing, playing board games, or playing video games. Downloading books and movies, or having a DVD player and a movie library to go with it, are great ways to ensure you're your kids will have plenty to do when you're on long passages.

But sailing kids are also part of sailing families and providing them with lots of entertainment is only part of the solution. Taj and Bella on *Catalpa*, Darry, Yewan and Rowan on *Mothership*, and Katie on *Ros Ailither* all contribute to passage making by taking night watches (building up slowly, with a parent resting close by), by helming and adjusting the sails and rigging when needed, and by cooking and doing other chores. Giving them roles and responsibilities appropriate to their age will make them more likely to take ownership of the passage.

These cruising years and cruising experiences are still in the future for *La Vagabonde III*. I'm excited to see how Lenny and Darwin grow and develop, learn and make friends over the next few years.

Tips:

- There are multiple approaches to educating your children. Mix and match and create a learning environment that suits your family.

- Establish an educational routine for numeracy, literacy, and other subject areas that you want to focus on – first thing in the morning is best.

- Don't try to recreate a school environment. Keep it short, mix it up, and turn it on its head if it's not working.

- Remember that all kids have unique learning styles and develop at different rates.

- Make your kids' friendships a priority – happy kids, happy boat.

Chapter 6

Sailing with teens

"My friend says sailing life for teenagers is full of really high highs and really low lows," says Rowan. Not too different to the lives of most teenagers, then. Rowan, who's now 17, cruised with her family from the age of 11 to 16. Most of us remember the intensity of friendships in our teenage years, as we increasingly exerted our independence from our parents, and when we started to think about leaving home.

It all seems a long way away for Lenny and Darwin, but I know in just the blink of an eye they'll be on that rollercoaster of teenage life. Many cruising families return to life on land before or when their kids are in their early teens, mostly because of education. But there remain quite a few families out there who have continued to cruise throughout their kids' teenage years and some who have set sail for the first time with teens. It's true that the community is not as large as that of families with younger kids. That can be a challenge at a time in most kids' lives when they want to spend more time with friends than with family. Cruising with teenage kids is all about growing independence, friendships, education, and spreading their wings as they prepare to leave home.

Growing independence

Fighting your kid's growing independence is a surefire way to make for an unhappy existence for everyone living in your small home. Teenagers on boats are no different to teenagers anywhere else; although, as Rowan says, "It's weird, because you're pushing different boundaries on a boat." Cruising kids, in general, spend a great deal more time with their parents than other kids tend to. Their parents are their teachers and their carers; they are also the people they go on adventures with, and they are their crewmates. In addition, given the nature of cruising, most kids don't have many long-term in-person friendships (although, as we've seen, friendships can be sustained over great distances). Therefore, the relationships that cruising teenagers have with their parents are often based on common experiences, a sense of being on a big adventure together, and relying on each other. So, as Rowan says, the boundaries that cruising teenagers push are different.

Teenagers have a growing sense of themselves as individuals distinct from their parents and from their home life. Acknowledging and making room for that growing independence will make life aboard a whole lot more pleasant for everyone. This growing independence doesn't always come easy. Sara says there's a lot more

Bella and Taj *(Catalpa II)*

tension onboard now than when Taj and Bella were younger. "But you learn coping mechanisms," she says, "and, at the end of the day, we all really like each other."

Space

One important coping mechanism is giving your teens space, both in their heads and in their surroundings. Easier said than done in the small confines of a boat and if you're travelling in places that are new or unfamiliar to you. Of course, giving teens space doesn't mean giving them free rein to do what they want; they're still your kids and you're still the skipper. But if you look for it, you'll find ways to make and give space.

At some point, your teenager is going to want their own space on board – be that a cabin or some other space that they can put a physical boundary around to make their own. When they first moved aboard *Catalpa*, Bella and Taj shared the V-berth. But daily bickering of the 'She's/He's touching my side' variety, meant that a space solution was called for, and Bella moved into the quarter berth, with a curtain for privacy, a common – if not ideal – solution on many monohulls. "It's not that they didn't want to be together," Sara says. "They each just wanted their own place where they could be alone when they needed to be." Recently, the family moved from 44ft *Catalpa* to 53ft *Catalpa II*. "My cabin is massive," Bella says. "And I have a door! We all have our own space now and it doesn't feel like we're up in each other's business all the time."

Finding space might mean sharing space. Aboard *Mothership*, Rowan's bedroom was also the quarter berth. "I couldn't just go to my room, because it's the corridor," she says. Her parents' cabin, which had long been her study space, owing to its built-in desk, became her de facto place of refuge. "If I shut the door, that meant I wanted time alone," she says. "If I wanted to call my friends or if I needed to get away from everyone for a little bit, I'd try to put myself in that little place." While her brothers didn't always respect her need to be alone, the closed door was a sign that she was seeking solitude.

Space on board isn't always available. Passage making or poor weather conditions might mean you are all stuck together. Throw in an extra crew member or part of the boat being out of bounds for repairs, and suddenly you are all, to quote Bella, 'up in each other's business.' Still, you can respect your teen's need for space simply by ignoring them. Having their ear buds in, or burying their face in a book or in a tablet are all signs that your teen needs some alone time. Give it to them. Life onboard will be all the calmer for it.

While your boat might be small, the world around it is not. Teenagers and adults alike can create space for themselves by simply getting off the boat: getting into the water for a swim; getting out on the water with a rowboat, kayak, or SUP board; going for a walk on a nearby beach. The options for getting away from everyone else on board, while staying close by, are almost endless. Trust your teen. Most aren't going to do anything crazy or dangerous. They just want head space and to spread their wings a little bit.

Some cruising parents feel upset when, having dropped anchor, packed a picnic, and made a plan to go ashore, their teenager decides they don't want to go. Do you fight with them, cajole them, beg them to go? Surely, you haven't sailed half way around the world for your kid to stay on the boat with their head buried in a book or a video game? But consider this: if you were living in a house, your teenager wouldn't want to hang out with you 24/7, doing all the things that you do, and being in your company all the time. Your boat's no different. "It's the hardest thing, living with someone 24 hours a day," Hazel said, recalling teenager Katie's increasing reluctance to go on family excursions off the boat in their final year living aboard. Indeed, after hours, days, or even weeks together at close quarters, your teenager is probably relieved that you're leaving the boat and giving them a few hours of peace and quiet. So, why not do everyone a favor, leave your teen aboard if that's where they want to be, and take a break from each other.

"It's mostly about communication," Rowan says. "Telling your family when you want some time alone." That's one half of it; the other is listening to and respecting that desire for time alone.

Decision-making

As your kids develop and mature, including them in cruising decision-making is more important than ever, giving them a greater sense of ownership and belonging to the journey you are on. Aiming to be more Ernest Shackleton than Captain Ahab will make for a more enjoyable life for everyone. Given a voice, you might be surprised by the maturity of your teenager's thought processes and decisions.

Having spent more than three years in the Mediterranean, where cruising teenagers are in short supply, *Mothership* crossed the Atlantic. Rowan was not happy. During a long-term stay at a marina in Spain, she had, at last, made friends with other cruising kids and was sad to leave them behind. Looking back, she says, "I was at an age where I wanted friends." Following their belief that finding other cruising kids is one of the three main drivers of their sailing choices, Woody and Irenka gave Rowan a choice to either set a course for the Caribbean islands, where she was sure to find other teenagers, or for Suriname. "My parents thought I wanted to go to the Caribbean because there are more kids there," Rowan says. "But I remember thinking Suriname is somewhere we'd probably never go again in my life. That made me feel very listened to and I enjoyed Suriname more because I felt that I hadn't been forced to go there. It was my decision."

However, not all kids like to make decisions and if your teen is more of a follow-the-lead type of person, then don't push it. Bella says, "They [her parents] always want our opinion. But I hate making decisions. I don't really mind where we go, so long as it's fun, has clear water, and there are things to do."

Spreading their wings

When your kids are little, they're with you, their other parent, or some other adult you trust, all of the time. Little by little, you become comfortable leaving them alone on the boat for short periods of time, or allowing them ashore to go to a specific shop or play area. Almost imperceptibly, their independence grows. Like kids everywhere, cruising teens want to go out and explore the world on their own. Scary, right? Especially if you're in a place that you, as the adults onboard, are unfamiliar with.

Sara believes that giving kids lots of opportunities to observe how their parents behave in different and novel situations is key preparation for them gaining independence. "We spend so much time together as a family," she says. "They watch what we do and see how we interact with people." Bella and Taj's first steps into independently leaving the boat were trips to the market. "Always together," Sara says. "Lee and I have always been comfortable when they do things together – going to the market, walking down the road or to the beach, we've always allowed that in places that we've been in for a little while and that we know. We don't just let them wander in unknown places."

Their independence, and their parents' belief in them, has grown to the extent that, when they were in 14 and 16, together with another set of cruising siblings the same age, they asked to spend a night in a hotel in Lombok, Indonesia. Being boat kids, the four were excited to do things they hadn't experienced before – going to the movies and eating fast food with friends. Sara and Lee, though apprehensive, agreed to the plan and spent a sleepless night wondering how the four teens were getting on. They needn't have worried. The four had such a good time that they phoned their parents the next day and asked if they could stay another night, moving from the city hotel to a hotel by the beach. "They worked it all out for themselves," Sara says, making the booking and figuring out how to get there. "They had some learning moments, like when Taj couldn't remember his PIN number." After their initial apprehension, Sara and Lee were delighted that they had permitted the kids to do this. "You usually don't get to do all that stuff until you're older," Sara says.

While sending your mid-teen kids off to a city for a couple of days without an adult chaperone might be a step too far for you, there are many small steps you can take to respect your teen's need for greater freedom to explore the world on their own.

Personal safety

Remember those simple days when your personal safety worries were about dropping your toddler while transferring from boat to tender, or keeping your baby secure in heavy weather? Once your kids start exerting their independence and venturing further from home, you've got very different personal safety concerns to contend with. And while you can never ensure anyone's personal safety, there are a few things that cruising parents and newly independent teens can do to reduce risk.

- Scenario planning: Have regular conversations with your teen about their personal safety. Cruising in different places means that the risks and the situations your teen may find themselves in are always changing. Regularly discuss the possibility of different situations occurring, consider scenarios, discuss what your teen should do if they find themselves in those situations.

- Scout out new places together: When you anchor in a new place, make it a condition of your teen going out adult-free that they do a recce with you first. Together, take note of places such as the police station, safe public spaces, shops, and so on; and note places that should be avoided, if necessary.

- Have backup communication: Most teens have smartphones these days, but using them isn't always an option, particularly in places with poor internet/ phone service or if you're not on an expensive international calling plan. It's common for cruising teens to carry hand-held VHF radios as back-up, meaning they can be in contact with the boat or anyone else in VHF range. Check the range of your hand-held VHF, and set distance boundaries for your kids.

- Stick together: Most cruising parents take a 'safety in numbers' approach, and make exploring ashore conditional on their teen always being in the company of siblings, friends, or other known and trusted individuals.

Despite having generally carefree and positive experiences, Rowan found herself in a couple of scary situations (in one of which the threat came from corrupt police) in one South American country. She feels that, although those experiences were scary, being in a group with other cruising teens, standing their ground, and refusing to leave a public place when told to, all reduced the danger they were in.

Friendship

"It doesn't matter where you go, in the end, kids are happier with other kids," Irenka says. "When they're younger, it doesn't matter so much. But when you have older kids who want to socialize, you have to plan for that if you're going to make [cruising life] work." At no other time in life are friendships as intense as during the teenage years. But is it possible for cruising teens to have the depth and breadth of friendships that most crave?

Developing friendships

It's true that there aren't as many cruising teenagers as there are kids of other ages. But they are there, particularly in the Caribbean, which is an important cruising ground for many American families.

One thing that cruising kids of all ages, and teens in particular, have in common – they make friends fast. "No matter your background or if you don't fit very well," Rowan says, "you always make friends, because you all know there aren't that many other kids out there." Such friendships can move from just met to deep friendship in a very short space of time. With two or more families anchored close by, friendship can develop out on the water or on the nearest beach. "I've had friends that, after only knowing them a few hours, we were already having a sleepover at our boat or theirs," Rowan says. Taj says "You make a different connection with people when you're sailing. Some people you meet on land and you still might not know them well after weeks or months. But you meet people when you're sailing and you only know them for three days, but it feels like you've known them longer."

As I noted in Chapter 5, such intense friendships can end just as quickly, with one friend setting sail soon after meeting, perhaps never to be seen again. Friendships color the experiences that teens have in places. Rowan says that although she "absolutely loved" the Mediterranean, the general lack of other teenagers made it a lot less fun. "It can never compare to doing things with kids my age," she says. Meanwhile, memories of many of her experiences in the Caribbean islands and the Caribbean coast of Central and South America are colored by the friends she met there. "It was what I had expected life on the boat would be like – paddle boarding at 5am, going out with other teenagers, having fun."

Facilitating your teen's friendships

How much time your teen gets to spend with other kids is, of course, entirely up to you. If I suggested you slow down to make sailing with a baby or toddler more enjoyable and comfortable, then slowing down with a teenager will allow them to develop friendships with other kids.

After the general lack of opportunities for their kids to make friends in the Mediterranean, Woody and Irenka realized they would have to be prepared to change their plans, even changing the countries they planned to go to, if it made the circumnavigation better for the children. As a result, they have stayed in some places, such as Martinique, longer than planned. "Rowan was happy because she had a teenage group," Irenka says.

In the early days of cruising, many families are shy about buddying up with other cruisers, thinking they might be cramping their style or getting in their way. But if you meet a family whose company you all enjoy, why not suggest hanging out together for a while. That might be a few days or a few weeks. The *Catalpa* family cruised for an entire year with a family they met in Indonesia, the two yachts often rafted together at anchor, and the two families regularly went on excursions and hung out together. They have, at other times, buddied with families for weeks or months at a time.

In short, if there are opportunities for your teen to socialize with other teens, or if you can find ways to put your family in the way of such opportunities, then grab them. This adventure belongs to the entire family. Do you need to tick every place off your sailing bucket list? Or can you hang out some place for an unplanned few weeks or months, or change course, or buddy up with someone else, if it will bring joy to your teenager, facilitate a friendship, and create lasting positive memories?

Maintaining friendships

As I noted in the previous chapter, it is far easier for older cruising children to maintain friendships with kids they've met along the way. Not only are they digital and social media experts; they've reached an age where friendships are less about playing together (online gaming excepted) and more about talking and sharing thoughts and ideas.

Cruising teens have their own friends' groups on messaging and social media platforms, and they follow and comment on each other's posts on Instagram, TikTok, and whatever other platforms teens are using these days. Rowan is in a group with friends she met four years ago. Those friends sail all over the world, and the group continuously expands to include new friends met along the way. "There are friends of friends on there now that I've never met," Rowan says. "It's really global."

Rowan says that, due to the nature of the lives they live, the sailing teens in her social media groups understand that if someone doesn't reply to a message for a few days or even weeks, then they're likely passage making or otherwise lacking access to the internet. "Everyone understands," she says. Since moving to the UK to continue her education, she has found that her friend group at school is much more impatient and it can be quite a big deal if she doesn't respond to messages for a few days.

"We have the same problems everyone has," Rowan's mum says. "Too much screen time; too much gaming." However, for Rowan and her brothers, much of that time is spent keeping in touch with live aboard friends spread throughout the world.

While keeping in touch via their phones is second nature to most teens, Taj says that, for him, the biggest downside of the life he leads is not having a friend to hang out with who he's known for years. He and his sister have formed deep friendships with other cruising teens, but they are not present in their lives on a regular basis; indeed, most of the friends they have are only physically present for a short period of time before becoming online friends.

Finding friends is definitely a challenge, depending on where in the world you are cruising, and creating, as Rowan said, 'high highs and low lows.' Being aware of this can make it more bearable for parents and teens, and using apps such as SeaPeople and Facebook groups can certainly increase your chances of finding and spending time with other boats with teenagers aboard.

Education

Parents worry especially about being unable to educate their teenage kids owing to their advanced level of study. How on earth will you help your kid with high school level maths, science, foreign languages, native language and literature, history, geography? If you're lucky, you might be confident in one or two subject areas. Not many of us have a rounded knowledge of *everything* on a typical high school curriculum.

The thing is, you don't need to know everything. During adolescence, cruising teens tend to transition from home schooling to unschooling or being self-taught, with their education increasingly being led by their own interests, what they feel they need to know, or what is required for formal state exams, if they choose to sit them. Therefore, as a parent of a teen, think of yourself more as a facilitator, providing them with the space, time, resources, and encouragement to learn. Of course, there will be times when they get stumped, when polynomials make no sense, when the Spanish subjunctive is just too confusing, or when Planck's constant gives them a headache. Most parents find they have two choices – attempt to learn it with and alongside their teen, or seek help from someone who knows this stuff.

Homeschooling to unschooling

If you and your teenage kid are new to cruising, you might be thinking, 'Unschooling is all well and good for kids who've grown up on boats. They're used to alternative education. My kid's not going to know how to self-teach.' You might be surprised. When Juliana and Valentin set sail with their four boys aboard *Argo*, Arvin, then 14, decided he wanted to spend the year away focusing on the school subjects he liked. His parents gave him free rein to explore on his own. "He's really focused on maths and chemistry," Valentin says. "He seeks out new topics and works through them for himself." Like many older kids, Arvin's most important educational resource is his tablet, which he uses to watch educational videos on YouTube that explain maths and chemistry problems.

Valentin is confident that when Arvin returns to school at the end of their cruising sabbatical, he will have an advantage over his classmates in those subjects. But his mum believes that his experience of unschooling will have benefitted him in other ways too. "In the year before we set sail, he'd developed a very strong sense of following the rules," Julianna says. "This year of breaking out of that, and following his own instinct is a very good experience for him." Despite focusing on maths and chemistry during his year away from school, his parents believe this positive learning experience will benefit him in all subjects, in deciding for himself what and how to learn, with no-one telling him what he should be doing.

If you have confidence (even a little) in your teen to unschool or to be self-taught, allow them the freedom to spend as much time as they want learning about what it important to them. Their commitment and dedication to the thing they're passionate about might surprise you. Rather than studying a subject they love for only two hours a week, why not give them the freedom to study it for as many hours as they want. If your kid, like Arvin, loves chemistry, why force them to study other subjects that don't interest them? This is a formal education mindset that many parents struggle to rid themselves of.

Aboard *Mothership*, Rowan went from a loosely structured home education curriculum to being almost completely self-taught. This transition emerged from her frustrations at her parents not always knowing the answers to her questions and their suggestions that they try to figure it out together. "She hated that," Irenka says. "She wanted a teacher. She didn't like it when I didn't know something." Instead, she turned to the internet for answers and made the transition to being self-taught.

Rowan admits to preferring a more structured approach to education. In her final year aboard *Mothership*, she chose to enroll in an online GCSE science course and completed projects of her own design for sociology and business.

Sara admits that home schooling wasn't always easy. "Taj and I would fight all the time," she says. "Every day I'd beg him – just do your work, just half an hour, get it done." She says she often bribed him with promises of spearfishing or surfing to get him to finish his work. She admits to putting pressure on herself, wanting to feel that she was educating her kids the 'right way.' Taj, however, had other ideas. By the age of 14, he already knew what he wanted to do. A budding artist, he wanted to improve his drawing skills, learn about different drawing techniques, and figure out how he could make money from his art. "I was still pestering him to do maths and social science," Sara says. But Taj made a strong case for why he should be left alone to follow his own interests. "I told my mum and dad," he says, "'I want to spend time doing what I love. Why memorize something from history when I could be refining my skill set on what I love doing?'" Eventually, after some persuasion, Sara and Lee decided to give Taj the freedom to learn what and how he wanted. Taj is now 17 and has been self-educating for almost three years, listening to podcasts, reading, and practicing his craft. He watches YouTube videos to learn how to draw, how to use Photoshop illustrator, and how to design software. "It was a relief," Sara says, "to see that he could handle it."

Taj is now making money through his business, Art of Taj.[12] From designing t-shirt logos and creating paintings for people, he says he's now "leveraging out" – "I'm leaning towards licensing

---

12   https://www.instagram.com/artoftaj/?hl=en

my work with certain companies, so that I'll have a royalty share whenever a company uses my logo." Smart kid!

However, no two children are the same, even in the same family, even on the same boat. While Taj was sure of what he wanted to do and how he wanted to do it by the age of 14, his younger sister, Bella, now 14, is following a different path. "She's not as self-driven," Sara says, and she continues to study maths and English with her mum every day. She has, however, taught herself to play the guitar and ukelele and to cook; and, in the past year, she's discovered the joys of reading for pleasure. "She's at a point now where she's starting to self-learn," Sara says.

Sara admits that she and Lee have had to learn to let their kids' education unfold. "Our kids are very different people and they learn in different ways. Taj has been unschooling for three years now and Bella's moving in that direction too."

Have confidence in your teen. Talk to them. Discuss what they want out of education. Maybe they still want you to be hands on. Or maybe they want you to leave them to it. Whatever their needs, facilitate that as much as you can.

Formal education and examinations

At 16, Rowan left her parents and brothers in Tahiti and flew back to the UK to attend school. "We were going to get her to sit her [UK state exams] in New Zealand, so we could carry on sailing together," Irenka says. However, Rowan realized her more structured approach to learning was better suited to a formal school environment. Her grandmother, who has always been skeptical of her grandchildren's home education, thought so too, and was very happy for Rowan to live with her while she completed her secondary studies.

From an educational perspective, Rowan says she is a lot more self-motivated than some of her peers at school, but not quite as much as she thought she'd be. "Obviously, I'm still a teenager, so sometimes I'd rather lie in bed than do the work," she says.

The mid-teenage years are a time when parents and teens often become more preoccupied with measuring educational progress against school or exam standards. For teens who want to enter college or university, this can be particularly important. If taking exams is important to you or your teen, or if exam scores are required for your teen's next steps in education, bear in mind that you don't have to return to your home country to sit exams.

- Some countries, such as the UK and the US, have test centers in many countries around the world, where students can register to sit exams such as GCSEs, A Levels (UK), and SATs (US).

- Some countries, such as Ireland, allow individuals to register as independent students to sit state exams at a test center in that country. While this requires your teen to be in that country for the exam, it does not require them to be registered as a student in a school.

- Universities that set their own entrance exams may offer the option to sit those exams under exam conditions elsewhere. Speak to the university of your choice to see what provisions they offer.

However, it's important to know that there are multiple ways to be accepted into higher education. Just because most students follow the exam route doesn't mean it's the only route. Many universities offer alternative options for non-traditional students, including entrance exams, extended essays, interviews, proof of completion of accredited and recognized online courses, proof of relevant experience and skills, and so on.

If your teen wants to pursue a particular higher education path, do the research, contact the college or university, and find out what your kid needs to do (including alternatives) to be accepted.

You may be surprised to find that you have options that don't involve sitting a formal exam and bringing your sailing adventure to an end just yet.

Leaving home

Inevitably, your teen will spread their wings and leave home. I've met cruising families with kids who've moved from their family boat onto their own boat and are now following their own sailing dreams. I've also met cruising families whose kids moved ashore at the first opportunity, seeking the most conventional land-fast life they could. Most kids fall somewhere between those two extremes.

Taj, now 17, has started to make solo forays off *Catalpa*, exploring the world on his own for a week or two at a time. "He's not stupid," Sara laughs. "He knows how much it costs to feed himself, so he's going to stay around a little longer." For the time being, both Bella and Taj are happy to remain at home, especially as the new boat has given them greater space and more sailing options. Bella has no desire to go to university unless it is to study for a specific career, such as to become a doctor. Taj, meanwhile, is averse to the debt incurred by going to university. Instead, he is focused on building his art business. "I want my income to enable me to work wherever I am in the world," he says. "I don't want to be tied to one location or rely on someone in one place. I want to go wherever I want, whenever I want."

Rowan, meanwhile, has left home. Irenka misses having her aboard. "I wanted her to stay," she says, "but I had to remind myself that there were lots of times in recent years when she didn't have kids her own age around. I always felt bad when she didn't have that." Irenka admits that life is perhaps a little easier for everyone now. "Now we just try to find cruising families with kids the same age as our boys," Irenka says, referring to the difficulty of finding cruising kids across a wider age spectrum when Rowan was aboard.

Rowan, meanwhile, has a group of friends her own age and is finding academic fulfilment. "She was sort of muddling through before," Irenka says, "trying to teach herself with our support. She didn't find the work difficult, but it was difficult not having friends and difficult learning on her own."

Back in the UK and living with her grandmother, Rowan makes a call to *Mothership* most evenings. During those calls, she seeks her parents' advice and assistance, swaps music and streaming recommendations with her parents and brothers, and chats to her brothers about their day. "It sometimes makes me homesick," she says. "It makes me think, 'if I were there now….'." The large and often-changing time difference is a challenge, as her family continues to sail west on their circumnavigation. When they are passage making, she can be out of contact with them for days or more at a time, and follows their progress by reading the brief text updates they post on their navigation app. "I can read between the lines in those a little bit," she says. "I can see if things are going well or if my parents are having a dig at each other."

For cruising parents who have allowed their children those incremental steps to independence, moving off the boat will merely be one more step. It may be quite a big step, if your teen is moving to the other side of the world and, owing to your sailing plans and their study/work/travel schedule, you don't know when you'll see them again. But your kids have grown up comfortable with using social and digital media apps to keep in contact and maintain relationships with people they have come to care for all over the world. They'll know what to do.

Tips

- Respect your teen's need for space and find ways to create emotional, psychological, and physical spaces on and off the boat.

- As your teen becomes more independent, have regular discussions about their safety, work through risky or dangerous scenarios, and devise action plans.

- Consider your teen's need for friends and be willing to alter your plans if it means they can develop friendships with other cruising teens.

- Explore and be open to multiple paths your teen can take to achieve their educational or other goals. Success doesn't necessarily mean a college degree; pursuing a college degree doesn't necessarily mean sitting formal exams.

Part II

It's early 2024, and we've just moved aboard our new home, La Vagabonde III. *It's taken us three years to have her built and, even though we've moved aboard and she's had some sea trials, she's still not ready. On our shakedown sail to Malaysia, the brand-new diesel engine was destroyed by salt water intrusion. Still under warranty, the engine's been removed and we're waiting for a replacement. That too is taking longer than expected.* La Vagabonde III *is new and shiny and beautiful and so different to her predecessor and we're still getting used to the new layout of the galley, our new living and sleeping spaces, all of her special features. It's early morning, and I've already been for a run. Riley is syncing up our new battery system. Lenny and Darwin have had breakfast and are doing half an hour of online interactive learning on their iPads. I'm on hand to help when they get stumped, while I put the breakfast stuff away, still not used to where everything goes. When the boys go ashore for a few hours with Ellie (our crew member whose responsibilities include watching over the boys, and heling with the cooking and cleaning), I get straight down to work. There are emails to reply to, my Instagram account to curate, and now it's time for*

Riley and me to shoot content for our YouTube channel. Today, it's a tour of our new home. Riley films me doing the tour of the inside, domestic parts of the boat, and then I film him doing sailing and techy stuff. Our new crew, Forrest, helps out with shots and ideas. Shooting the videos is fun but full-on — Sailing La Vagabonde *is my full-time job and business after all — and the new angles and lighting are yet more things to get used to on the new boat. The boat tour shots filmed, Riley and I take a quick trip out in the tender to run some final test trials for our new SeaPeople app. The boys are already home when we get back and Ellie has started to prepare lunch, which all six of us sit down to eat together. Mid-afternoon is family time, and we're off to a gorgeous beach we've discovered a few miles away. I film a little, but Riley and I have been working all morning and we'd rather just hang out with the boys. We swim and explore, and the boys tell us about their morning. It's all a welcome break from our hectic morning. All too soon, a couple of hours have passed and it's time to head for home and showers, supper, winding down time, and bed. It's Riley's turn to read the bedtime story tonight. I sit out on deck, breathing deeply while I watch the setting sun.*

Family cruising is a joyful and magical way to live. But it doesn't happen in a vacuum. At the same time as living the life of your dreams, loving and supporting your children through whatever stage of life they're at, and exploring the world by sea, the rest of life is going on around you. Your boat — you home, office, school room, mode of transport, and so much more besides — needs your constant care and attention. And, unless you've hit the jackpot, you need to earn a living to finance this fabulous life you're living. There are

Fresh provisions *(La Vagabonde II)*

bills to pay, plans to make, decisions to be made. All of this takes time and requires mental and physical space. Time is always in short supply when you have kids and space is always in short supply when you live on a boat. So, how do you make it work?

This second part of the book explores boat life more generally. I look at the time spent working, both to repair and maintain your boat and to earn a living, in a small space and having your kids with you pretty much all the time. There are fantastic online and offline resources to guide you through boat maintenance and repair and to inspire you and offer ideas and guidance for nomadic and digital work. I won't repeat those here. Rather, the other families and I offer insights into the time and financial costs of sailing, and how to negotiate work so that it fits your family life. In this part of the book, I also look at caring for the mental and physical health of everyone onboard and I offer insights into making a smooth transition from boat back to land. Most of all, this part of the book demonstrates the various ways you can make cruising as a family work on your terms and will give you the confidence to live this life exactly the way you want.

Chapter 7

Your floating home

Oh, the places you'll go! You have big dreams to explore the world with your family over the course of a few months, a year or two, or indefinitely. Trust me, you're going to have unforgettable experiences. But there will be times when your carefully laid plans fall apart. Delays in paperwork, unexpected boat maintenance and repairs, and you find yourself sitting in a boatyard, your hands covered in engine grease, wondering if it's all worth it. I'm here to tell you: it is.

In this chapter and the next, I want you to encourage you to alter your cruising mindset, from one where your expectations are for Instagram perfection, to a reality that is much messier. A major reality of cruising life is the time, effort, and money you have to devote to your boat. Rather than viewing boat repair time (this chapter) or work time (Chapter 8) as lost time, I want you to think about those times as part of the process. Instead of thinking about the time spent sitting in a boat yard, or when all you see of your partner from morning to night is their bum sticking out of the engine compartment, as time when you should/could be sailing, think of that as an integral part of your cruising life. Slow down. Embrace the times when you must prioritize work. Find ways to create space for each other to work and to relax during those times. Don't sit in rainy Plymouth wishing you were cruising in French Polynesia. Look around you at all the play and education opportunities on your doorstep. Your kids won't care where they are, because everywhere is a new adventure for them.

This is your life, not your vacation

If you're moving aboard a sailing boat for the first time – or even if you're moving back onboard having been away for a while, it's hard not to feel as if you're on vacation. You're living on a boat, for goodness' sake! You wake up each morning surrounded by the sea, free to do what you want, your schedule dictated by the wind, weather, and tides, rather than school, public transport timetables, and work schedules. Ah, the freedom!! And the incomparable sense of elation because this is your life!! Even the cruising kids who contributed to this book admitted that in the early days of sailing, they found it hard to do school work, because life felt like one long vacation. Such a great feeling!

However, if you want to carry on with this lifestyle that you've dreamed about and planned, you need to change your mindset from that initial vacation feeling to understanding that this is your full-time life. And what an incredible full-time life it is. But, even more so than living in a house, there will always be boat maintenance and repairs to do. Unexpected boat costs will inevitably pop up (the result of general wear and tear or an unexpected accident). Successful family cruising ultimately comes down to being in the right frame of mind, forming habits, and embracing cruising as your life and not your vacation.

Choosing the 'right' boat

I'm sometimes asked what's the best boat for family cruising. My answer is simple: there isn't one. Obviously, you want a boat that's seaworthy. I'd recommend comfort over speed – if you can find or build a boat with both, you've hit the jackpot. Unless you have

149

a bespoke build, no boat will be a perfect match for your needs. Indeed, once you set sail on your bespoke boat, you're probably going to discover things that you wish you'd done differently.

There is no perfect shape or size. The families who contributed to this book live on boats of a variety of sizes, ages, styles, and shapes. Most monohull families live on boats of more than 40 feet, but some live happily on smaller boats. However, no matter the size or design of your boat, there are certain features that make cruising with smaller children a lot easier. But let's face it, most boats aren't designed to be family homes and often you have to take what you can get, based on your budget and what's on the market. This book is not about finding the ideal boat for cruising. You'll find lots of advice online about good family cruising yachts. But there are some features that will make your life easier and make for smoother sailing.

- Internal access between all parts of the boat. With small children, in particular, being able to get from your cabin to theirs without having to go up on deck is ideal.

- Avoid an open transom to enhance safety at the back of your boat.

- A deep centre cockpit will provide greater protection from the elements and keep little ones off deck.

- A companionway that isn't too steep, so that children (and parents carrying children) can safely climb in and out of the saloon.

However, many families live on boats with few or none of these features and still make it work. No boat is built with kids in mind (now there's a business opportunity!). So, take your time to find the boat that's right for your family. Yachting and cruising organization websites have checklists and guidelines to help you choose the right boat. Help is also at hand in the form of professional boat buyers.

(Above: *Tranquillity*)
(Below: *Ros Ailither)*

Few boats are perfect and families make do. Bart, Kim, and Liz live aboard 33ft *Tranquillity*, which they admit has two disadvantages. For 1.95m Bart, there is no headroom anywhere below deck (although his berth is 2m in length) and the boat is a cruiser-racer, so not built for blue water cruising. Despite these drawbacks, the couple decided to sail it from the Netherlands to the Caribbean. "We had long discussions about whether to buy a more appropriate boat," Bart says. In the end, their decision to stay aboard *Tranquillity* came down to two things: (a) it left them with more money, so they could cruise for longer and (b) they'd already done a lot of work on her. "If anything went wrong," Bart says, "I already knew her well." So, they decided to make some adjustments to make her more suitable for long-term family cruising.

Likewise, Sara and Lee never intended to sail the world aboard *Catalpa*. They prepared her for sale and intended to buy a more appropriate cruising yacht. "It was a lot of work," Sara says. "By the time we fixed her up, we realized that maybe we could sail her around the world." So, they spent what they could afford preparing her for family cruising. Remember, turning your boat into a blue water cruiser can be expensive. The water maker and wind generator (and a new rudder) that we installed on the first *La Vagabonde* were big ticket items that really ate into our savings.

Your beloved money pit
Become the expert of your own boat

Let's get one thing clear. Most yachts are not built to have people living on them full-time. They're built for leisure, for occasional use, for fun. They're not meant to be full-time homes that double up as home offices, workshops, classrooms, laboratories, and infirmaries. And yet, for those of us who live aboard full-time, they are all those things. All that use, before you even consider the impact of sailing and simply being in the water, quickly causes your boat to deteriorate. One thing every yachtie will tell you – your boat will require constant and never-ending maintenance.

The amount of maintenance will depend on (a) the age and condition of your boat, (b) the amount of use it gets, and (c) sheer luck. Living aboard and sailing full-time causes a lot of wear and tear and regular ongoing small amounts of maintenance, in a lot of cases, avoids the need for bigger repairs, or prolongs the life of parts and equipment. However, things can happen that are beyond your control – an unmarked submerged rock, another boat, unexpected or unavoidable foul weather – causing major damage that can require a great deal of money and time to repair. Even if your boat is insured (and you should have insurance, but read the small print carefully), if your boat is also your home, you may not be able to wait the months it might take for your insurance payment to come through before you start making the necessary repairs.

The biggest favor you can do for yourself is learn to do all or most of your boat's regular upkeep and its less regular repairs. "If you or your partner don't know how to fix everything on board, then you're going to need a lot of money," Sara says. "You're going to have to pay people to do it, and that'll cost you a fortune."

Does that mean you have to be an engineer-plumber-electrician to run a boat? Not at all; although it kind of helps to teach yourself to be a little bit of all of those. "When we first got *Carina*," Martina recalls. "Julian spent so much time watching YouTube videos, learning how to make boat repairs. The sea cocks wouldn't move, the nav light wiring was a mess, the anodes needed to be replaced. There was a YouTube video for everything." Learning to do all that stuff yourself is time-consuming. But it will save you money and allow you to get intimately acquainted with the workings of your boat. "There will be times," Sara says, "when you'll be in places where there are no professionals or experts to fix the problem for you. You'll have no choice but to do it yourself."

Aboard *La Vagabonde*, Riley is responsible for the day-to-day and longer-term running of the boat, while I run the business (I'll return to that in Chapter 8). But it's really important that all the boat knowledge and skill doesn't reside in Riley's head only. We need to know that, in an emergency, or if Riley is unable to make a needed repair for some reason, that I can do it too. And it's never too early to get your kids involved in boat life, and to encourage them to learn maintenance and repairs. They too can contribute in age-appropriate ways (see below).

Maintenance is equal parts thought and action. Riley is constantly in maintenance planning mode. We sail in some remote places, where finding a well-stocked chandlery or a skilled expert isn't always an option. So, he plans ahead, making online purchases for parts we need, figuring out where they need to be mailed to, how long delivery will take, any other parts or tools needed to make the necessary repairs, planning our cruising route to coincide with those deliveries, and considering suitable anchorages or haul outs to make those repairs. I can almost see the cogs whirring in his brain ALL THE TIME. It's hard work. But the alternative is to not sail at all and/or pay a hell of a lot of money to have someone else do the repairs for us.

Embrace maintenance and repair time

No matter what you think, you are going to underestimate the length of time it will take to get your boat ready, and the amount of work it requires. Whether you have commissioned a new boat, like we just have, or you have bought a second-hand boat, as Riley did in the past, and all the other families in this book have done, the boat is going to take far longer to get ready than you think. "We bought the boat in Greece in 2017," Woody told me. "We hoped to simply launch it and sail off over the horizon." The reality, however, was quite different. "It needed a lot of repairs, so it took us a few years to get out of the Mediterranean." A few years! I kid you not. And Woody and

154

Irenka's experience is not unusual. So, if you're planning on buying a pre-loved boat and living on it with your kids, be aware that some (a lot) of that time will be spent in repairs. Even if you set sail early on, you might soon discover that your new home needs work. "We got the boat in July," Irenka recalls. "We moved out to Greece in October and spent a couple of months sailing there, thinking 'yeah, this is it.' Then, things started to fall apart." When the windlass crumbled as they reversed into Lefkas, the couple realized they had to prioritize repairs. For the next few years, they hopped around the Mediterranean, fixing up the boat and "muddling along." Woody says, "It brought us right down to the reality of what life on a boat is really like. It was a massive learning curve for those two years. It separated the dream from the reality."

YouTube boat repair channels

There are lots such YouTube channels out there, but it would be remiss of me not to shine the spotlight on both *Mothership*'s dedicated maintenance channel https://www.youtube.com/c/mothershipmaintenance, where Woody shows how he makes repairs on the move or when in places that lack supplies or reliable postal service, and *Catalpa*'s step-by-step videos of how they got *Catalpa II* ready to put to sea https://www.sailingcatalpa.com/catalpa-ii-project.

Even a new boat will take longer than you anticipate. There will be building delays, and then there's all the paperwork, and sea trials, and buying spare parts before you leave. Our sea trials of *La Vagabonde III* resulted in a sail ripping to shreds and the diesel engine completely corroding, adding many more weeks and many more headaches to getting her ready for blue water cruising. You're not going to simply drive your boat out of the showroom like you would a new car. I'm not telling you this to put you off. On the contrary. Get out there and do it. I just don't want you to be shocked or disappointed when preparing and repairing your boat takes a lot longer than you had anticipated.

It's easy to get annoyed with all those expected and unexpected boat tasks. They always take longer than anticipated and one job invariably leads to more, eating up more of your precious time and money. These jobs will take even longer when you have kids – especially younger kids – as one parent will need to be on full-time parenting duty while the other is working on the boat.

Try not to dwell on the blue water cruising you could be doing; instead, embrace this time in a boat yard/marina/anchorage as an inevitable and necessary aspect of cruising life. Look around. No matter where you are, you will find interesting and fun activities for your kids – playgrounds, beaches, museums, parks and gardens; play groups, libraries, homeschool family get-togethers; or simply getting to know and hanging out with other cruising families that come your way. Your kids will enjoy life no matter where they are, so long as you provide them with opportunities to run, play, and explore.

Time to call in the experts

There will be times when your expertise, and that of your friends and fellow yachties, runs out and you have to turn to an expert. That can be expensive. If possible, take the time to research financially optimal choices. When *Mothership* needed a new solar arch, for example, Woody and Irenka sailed from Spain to Tunisia, where the arch would be manufactured more cheaply. While there, in a less expensive boat yard, they took the opportunity to complete other big jobs, including repairing the bottom of the boat and fiber glassing. They then returned to Spain to overwinter, but sailed to Turkey the following spring, as it was the cheapest place in the Med to have new sails and rigging made. *La Vagabonde III* was built by the Australian-Canadian company Rapido, which is based in Vietnam where the costs of labor are lower. This meant that our costs around the build were less, including renting an apartment close-by. By our calculations, if she'd been built in Australia, the US, or Europe, she would have cost us up to three times what we actually paid.

All hands on deck

Preparing *Catalpa II* for cruising was a family affair. Taj and Bella sanded and painted and were responsible for the preparation of entire sections of the boat. Both teenagers say they are keen to reap the fruits of their labor, and feel emotionally invested in the boat because of the contributions they've made to getting her ready.

It is never too early to nurture your kid's participation in the life of your boat. It will only add to their and your enjoyment of the experience. Hazel says that they never really thought about nurturing Katie's and Reuben's interest in boat life. It simply happened organically. "We taught them how to row and paddle a kayak as soon as they were able. When we sailed, Katie always wanted to set up sails, look out for crab pots, help her dad out. We always believed the children should be involved and should help. It's good for their general life education that they all muck in." Yewan

Argo

says that, being the smallest on the boat, he's often called to help out. "The boat has so many small spaces where my parents can't fit their hands in, so I do it."

A day in the life of boat repairs

It feels like groundhog day aboard *Catalpa II*, which the Rice family has owned for six months. Currently in a marina in San Diego, the family has been working around the clock to refit her and prepare her for the open ocean. Today is a typical day. Lee, in the engine room since first light, is installing lithium batteries and sorting out the boat's electricity, while Bella varnishes supporting pieces of timber to go under the batteries. Taj is outside, removing the boat's old name, so she can receive her new name, *Catalpa II*. Sara, meanwhile, is at the saloon table, editing the family's latest YouTube video, an important source of income for the family. With the other three engaged in manual labor, Sara also has to make sure no-one gets hungry. The marina is expensive, and they're keen to get back on anchor as soon as possible. In addition, their US visas expire in two weeks, so *Catalpa II* must be ready for a sea-trial down to Mexico, where they will resume their work until she is ready to put to sea. "Wake up, look at the to-do list, get something done, get a little closer to getting out of here," Sara says.

Rather than treating your kids as passengers, think of them as active mini crew. Encouraging them to become mini crew will reap rewards in spades – for you and for them – and, who knows, one day it may even save your or their lives. Nurturing mini-crew requires two things. First, you need to slow down. Second, you need to be less precious about your boat. If you want your children to learn (and to want to learn) to care for their floating home, then you have to teach them how to do it at their pace and leave them to do it at their pace. And, be prepared for them to sometimes (often? always?) make a mess.

Irenka suggests getting kids involved in the running of the boat as early as possible. "Be patient with them," she says, "because things take a lot longer. Keep things simple." If you get them involved, she says, they'll rebel less. Start with small steps. Give them jobs that they can easily do and that will become 'their' jobs. Benjamin and Frank, aged 5 and 4, help to raise and lower the motor-assisted anchor, and take turns to turn on and off the engine. When *Sans Souci* comes alongside a pontoon, the boys help 'tidy up' the berthing lines. "They make a big mess," Jeroen laughs, "and are very happy and cheerful that they have helped me out." When Jeroen is doing woodwork onboard, he gives each of the boys a block of wood, a file and a screwdriver, so they can play around with those. "They're really happy that they're 'helping' with boat stuff," he says. "My girls loved cleaning the deck and the cockpit when they were little," Martina recalls. "They'd share a bucket of water and use sponges or brushes to clean."

And it's not just boat specific skills that you can nurture in your mini crew. Involve them in all aspects of live aboard life, such as cooking, cleaning, doing laundry, buying groceries, foraging for food, etc. Sure, each of these is guaranteed to be a slow and messy business when little kids are involved, but you and they will reap the rewards of knowing and appreciating the life they have, and learning important and life-long skills. These too are important contributions to family cruising life that can free you up to get on with maintenance and repair jobs and get you all back out on the water or onto the beach all the sooner.

One word of advice about nurturing mini crew. Don't be surprised if your little ones (no matter what age) have no interest in being out in the cockpit with you all day long when you're passage making. Just because you are moved by great expanses of wide-open ocean, doesn't mean your kids will care one whit for it. Rather than insisting that they spend all their time in the cockpit, let them do what they want. If they want to be below deck reading or playing with their Lego, let them be. If a pod of dolphins comes along or there's some amazing sight to see, call them up – chances are they'll want to see that. They'll enjoy the sailing experience all the more if it's not forced on them.

Tips

- No boat will have all the features you want. Do your research beforehand and know what features you want in your ideal boat.

- Embrace maintenance, repair, and other non-cruising time when you are caring for your boat as an integral part of cruising life. Look around – your kids will love life no matter where they are.

- Don't rush maintenance and repair work. Research your options. Can you make the repair yourself? If not, where can you get a good quality repair done for the best price? Once again, slow down.

- Mini crew: nurture your kids' natural curiosity about what you do, give them crew responsibilities that they can take pride in.

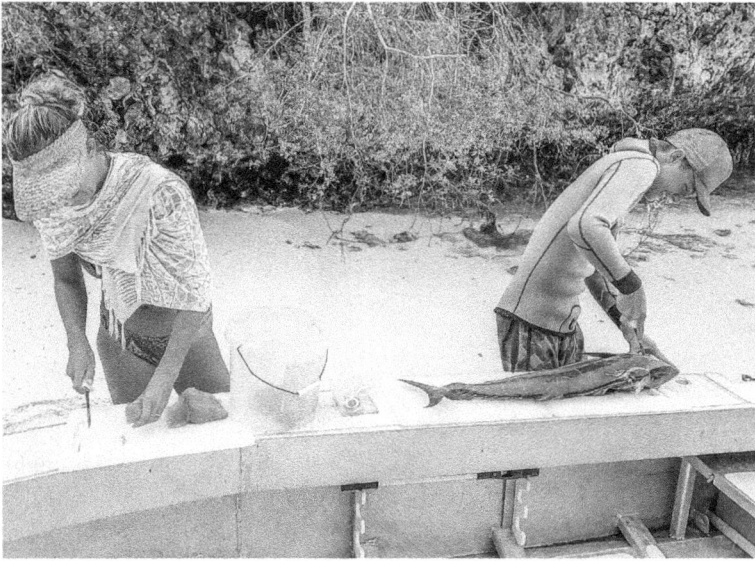

Getting involved – food prep
(Above: *Catalpa II)*
(Below: *Maes)*

Chapter 8

Work to cruise, cruise to work

When I first moved aboard *La Vagabonde* with Riley, I was shocked by how quickly we ploughed through our meagre savings. We might have been cruising in the Mediterranean, but we certainly weren't living a lavish Mediterranean yachting lifestyle. Far from it. We lived frugally, spent almost no money on ourselves, and lived on a diet of steamed vegetables and rice. It wasn't Riley and me who ate through the money, it was the boat. Sometimes, it felt like we were stuffing our money down the cockpit drain. In the previous chapter, I talked about boat maintenance and repair. Naturally, that comes at a financial cost. In this chapter, I will explore (a) how your expectations of family cruising will determine the financial costs of your lifestyle and (b) taking a hybrid approach to financing your boat and your cruising lifestyle.

I'm not going to beat around the bush here. The boat you sail on, which serves as your full-time home, mode of transport, office, and classroom, is going to eat up most of your budget in maintenance and repairs. It will cost you more than you think, and the costs never end. And when your boat is ready for action, you want to have the financial resources to explore and enjoy the places you visit.

But don't despair. Living aboard with your kids doesn't require super deep pockets. Sure, it helps, but most cruisers don't have super deep pockets (some don't seem to have any pockets at all!). Cruising families, for the most part, live in a completely different universe to

162

those millionaires on superyachts in Monaco and Cannes. "When I told my sister we were buying a yacht, she was so excited," Martina recalls. "She pictured herself lounging on the deck of my lavish yacht, champagne in hand, in the company of millionaire playboys. The reality of our cramped 36-foot Westerly Conway, where her accommodation was a sleeping bag in the saloon, came as a shock to her." That's more like real-life cruising for sure!

The financial costs of cruising, and continuing to cruise, can be challenging. Many are naïve about how much it will cost. The crew of *Catalpa* set sail with about AU$25,000 in the bank. Sara says, "We thought, 'we'll be good for a while'." However, they hadn't considered all the repairs needed. For the first six months, things broke all the time, which quickly ate into their savings. "I think it would be a lot less stressful if we had lots of money," Sara says, seven years on. "It makes it a lot harder when we always have to budget, always have to consider if we can afford to do certain things or be in certain places, or give as much as we want to our kids." Despite the challenges of cruising on a tight budget, cruisers find often novel ways to finance their family adventures. So, how do you cruise on a small budget with your family aboard your money eating home? Well, you cut your cloth to measure, as they say. The cost of cruising depends a lot on your boat, on your expectations, on where you cruise, and on whether you can continue to earn a living while cruising.

An important note: I have avoided including specific prices or costs in this chapter. First, every boat is different and maintenance costs vary depending on construction materials, boat size, and so on. Second, the cost of materials and hiring skilled labor can vary substantially by country or region and over time. Third, other expenses, such as country-specific taxes and anchoring/mooring/transit fees, are subject to change over time. Finally, each family sets sail from its own unique financial position. However, if you want to see examples of costs, both *Sailing Catalpa* and *Mothership Adrift* have produced blog and YouTube content about costs and how they finance them.

Making the most of your budget

Your boat will be, by far, the biggest drain on your bank balance. After that, it's easy to live an amazing cruising life on a limited budget. If you are frugal and adopt the 'this is not a vacation' approach, then you can stretch your money quite a long way. And the farther you stretch, the longer you can cruise. "The secret," Woody says, "is not so much what you buy, but rather what you don't spend."

Live simply

Unless you have deep pockets which, as we've already established, most cruising families don't, the key to successful long-term cruising is frugality. That doesn't mean going without. Instead, it means switching from that vacation mindset to a lifestyle mindset, living a simple life, and making the most of the amazing places you will, for sure, find yourself in. Simple, frugal living means eating well on less, taking advantage of free activities in the world around you, and making choices that cost less. By choosing to live well on less, you'll fill your cruising life with memorable experiences.

Eat well for less

There are supermarkets in most places these days where you can buy the same or similar foods to those you eat at home. However, they can be expensive, especially in more remote locations. Instead, adapt to the local cuisine and buy from local markets and street stalls, or from fishermen selling fresh fish from their boats. It took the crew of *Catalpa* a little while to adopt the mentality of eating well for less. At first, they continued to eat out and at home as they always had done. They soon discovered, however, that they could make their money stretch farther by changing their food buying habits. In Indonesia, the family started to live frugally off fish, rice, and vegetables. "The kids just learned that this was how we were going to live and it was either this or go back to the life we'd left behind," Sara says.

From day one, Riley and I have lived on simple meals of boiled rice, steamed vegetables, and fish that we catch ourselves, and that way of eating has continued with the boys. It's a very healthy diet and also incredibly varied as, every new place we sail to, we add different vegetables, fruits, and fish to our plates.

This approach to eating well for less can be extended beyond the boat to taking picnics when you go ashore or eating street food rather than in restaurants. These are also likely to be much more fun and memorable food experiences for your kids than going to some stuffy restaurant.

Remember, too, that most other cruisers (with or without families) are also living on tight budgets. So, rather than meeting up at bars or restaurants, suggest meeting on the beach or on each other's boats and bring your own, have a potluck, or cook a barbecue. It will all be a great food adventure.

Big adventures at a minimal cost

Adventure awaits at every turn and for little or no cost. It goes without saying that, in most instances, you can enjoy the sea right from your boat – swimming, snorkeling, free diving, rowing and, if you have the equipment on board, kayaking, dinghy sailing, SCUBA diving, and so on.

Once you're away from your boat, there are endless opportunities for inexpensive fun and adventure:

- Hiking is a free activity for everyone, except perhaps the very tiny. But if your kid is big enough to sit up in a back carrier, then a family hike is a great day out. "Once we reach a new anchorage," Irenka says, "we go walking. Everywhere in the world there are free trails." In addition to researching suitable hiking routes online, get information from other cruisers, locals, or tourist offices. For parents of young kids, a hike to the park or playground might be as far as you go.

- Lots of places in the world have free to enter museums, art galleries, and exhibitions. These might be national and regional or small and local. Either way, you're sure to learn something new. Martina says, "We've been to canneries-turned-shell-fishery museums, an old power station-turned-museum, churches with incredible sacred art. We've learned so many unexpected and memorable things just by visiting whatever free museums we come across."

- A library is a great place for kids to hang out. Apart from access to books, check the notice board or ask the librarian about free kid-friendly events.

- Don't overlook churches and other places of worship for kid-friendly fun. You don't have to be religious to join in play groups, events and activities, and kid-friendly coffee mornings for parents.

- If you're cruising in a home education-friendly part of the world, check out local home education Facebook or other groups, to join meet ups, excursions, and play dates.

Cruising costs

Depending on where you are in the world, you will also have to consider anchoring and mooring fees, marina fees, transit costs, such as the Panama Canal, and visitor fees, such as the Galapagos Islands. Do your research in advance, so that you are not hit with unexpected anchoring fees. "We didn't know we had to pay £5 a night to anchor in a river in southwest England until the harbor master came by in his boat the first morning," Martina says. "We were stuck there, making a repair to our engine," Martina says. "Imagine how delighted we were to finally cross to France and sail up a river with free moorings."

Financing your cruising lifestyle

Some families, particularly those who plan to cruise for a specific period of time, meticulously plan the cost of their trip in advance; others cruise by the seat of their pants. It all depends on your personality and what feels comfortable for you. Either way, financing your trip takes planning and patience, being open to learning and to unexpected possibilities that present themselves. But then, if you're already thinking that liveaboard family life might be for you, then I'm sure you'll be up for the challenge.

Hybrid approach

Gone are the days when blue water cruising meant saving up and using your life savings to fund a retirement at sea. These days, the post-COVID-19 and cyber technology realities of hybrid work and hybrid living means that most of us can continue to work as we cruise. Here, I explore some of the more common ways that cruising families earn their living.

Off-boat work

Home and away approach: Some cruising parents take a home and away approach to funding their lifestyle, setting sail for a year or two when they have saved up enough money and returning to their land-based life to fund the next trip. This is what Hazel and Dave did, continuing to live aboard *Ros Ailither* on her home mooring on the southwest coast of England and sending their children to school until they were ready for their next two-year cruise. For house owners, renting out your home for the duration of your cruise can be an added source of income while you are away.

Riley did this too, but on a much shorter time-scale. When we first met, he funded his (and then our) sailing life by returning to Western Australia for weeks at a time to work in the offshore oil and gas industry. While such on-and-off work is not ideal when you have a family, it can be a shorter-term solution. After five years cruising in Indonesia and Malaysia, Sara and Lee knew it was time for a new boat. Sara and the kids remained onboard in a marina in Langkawi in Malaysia, while Lee flew back and forth to Australia to work in mines to earn the money needed to buy a new boat. "The kids and I were comfortable staying there," Sara says. They had made friends with other families and were familiar with the local culture and language.

Seasonal employment: If you are sailing in parts of the world where the weather requires you to stay put for part of the year, you might be able to put your skills and qualifications to use locally. The crew of *Tranquillity* sat out hurricane season in Curaçao, where Bart worked as a nurse in a local hospital. Similarly, Martina taught English in a language academy when *Carina of Devon* overwintered in Spain. At the time of writing, Jessica and Jeroen plan to stay in the ABC Islands for a season or two. "Our budget isn't endless," Jessica said, "so we plan to work in Curaçao (which is a municipality of the Netherlands) for a while and put the children in school. Then maybe we'll do it again somewhere else the following year."

However, as Woody and Irenka discovered, it's not always easy to find work while cruising. While Irenka taught English for a while in Bocas del Toro, they have found fewer opportunities to work than they had expected.

Onboard work

Not even twenty years ago, onboard work for cruisers meant having a manual skill such as sail-making or engine repair. There are still mechanics, engineers, divers, and sail-makers out there who finance their live aboard lives by providing those services to other cruisers. Others support their lifestyle making and selling arts and crafts. These days, however, onboard work is open to pretty much any desk job and, of course, to digital creatives.

Over the past decade that we've been cruising, we've met architects, engineers, marketers, designers, clerical workers, editors, writers, all working while cruising. These jobs require reliable internet connection and having the space (both physical and mental) to do your work. The Starlink satellite system means that high speed internet is now available even in the remotest reaches of the Pacific Ocean; however, for the time being, it remains prohibitively expensive for many. Without it, there are parts of the world and on longer passages, when you are effectively cut off from the world for the purposes of online work.

A job that requires you to be in meetings or to meet strict deadlines can be a particular challenge, especially when you have kids on board. Valentin, Juliana, and their four sons are on a one-and-a-half-year cruising sabbatical around Europe. Valentin continues to work one day each week for his architectural firm in Germany. "That was the deal," he says. "I could go, but I had to be available one day a week for projects they need me on. That's also nice because it means my insurance is still covered."

Content creator: I didn't intentionally set out to make a living creating content. I started making videos soon after I joined Riley on the boat, simply because I enjoyed making videos. I posted one on YouTube every month or two to share with family and friends back in Australia. When the number of viewers started to grow and I realized that we could possibly earn a living doing this, I made it my mission to learn how to properly shoot, edit, and market my videos, and how to build a website and create merchandise. I worked full-time for four months, learning all I could about how to become a full-time YouTuber.

By the time Lenny was born, I'd already been creating content for a number of years. When we brought him home to *La Vagabonde* at seven weeks old, I went straight back to my full-on working life of creating content, shooting, editing, and posting videos, and maintaining my various social media platforms.

Creating content to earn a living is very time consuming. For most of my career as a content creator, shooting content was followed by 3–5 days of editing to transform the material into a quality video. I'd then spend another day taking a thumbnail, posting the video, and sharing it across all my platforms. As our channel grew, there were all the spin-offs, such as the merchandise and the books, and the marketing related to those. On top of that, my equipment needs lots of care. Laptops, hard drives, and camera equipment don't cope too well in the salty environment and with being bounced around the boat. I have the greatest job in the world, folks, but it's full-time and it's full-on. However, all those years of hard work have paid off. Over time, I've gradually built up a small team of people and now delegate most of the time-consuming editing work to them, leaving me with more free time to be with my boys.

An increasing number of family cruisers have taken the same content creator route. Of the families who have contributed to this book, those on *Catalpa*, *Mothership*, and *Sans Souci* are currently, or have in the past, financed their cruising, at least in part, through content creation.

Watching *Sailing La Vagabonde* and other YouTube channels gave Sara and Lee the idea to start their own *Catalpa* channel. "Initially, I thought it would be a record of what we were doing, for the kids to look back on in the future. Then I thought, 'Let's put this on YouTube and, who knows, something might happen.'" They developed a small following posting videos of fitting out *Catalpa* and then sailing along the east coast of Australia. When a little money started coming in – AU$1000 per month through Patreon – they realized that if they put the work in, it could contribute to financing

Above: Elayna *(La Vagabonde II)*

Below: Jessica, Jeroen, Frank and Benjamin *(Sans Souci)*

their voyage. "Our channel is still not big," Sara says. "But we make do. It was enough for us to live comfortably in Indonesia."

Jessica and Jeroen produced a regular Dutch-language vlog for a while, with Jessica editing videos for one and sometimes two full days per week, in addition to promoting it on multiple social media channels. "It was dedicated working time, when I was away from the children," Jessica says. "I locked myself in my cabin and worked on my bed all day. It was quite a challenge, but we had an unwritten rule that one day a week I would work." To stick to their schedule of uploading a new episode every week, Jessica usually worked for a couple of hours each evening too. Now that they no longer produce the vlog, Jessica wonders where she found the time to work on it. "At the time, our YouTube channel was our only source of income, so it was important," she says. "But if the work took more than two or three days a week, then it negatively impacted our travel, because we also needed time for boat maintenance," she says.

Jeroen says, "When we stopped making the vlog, we started to enjoy everything more. We started to live it for ourselves rather than being conscious that someone else would be watching what we were doing. Now we're living the moment more vividly."

In addition to income from subscribers and YouTube advertising revenue, many content creators receive sponsorship, in the form of 'free' stuff. Who doesn't love free stuff? It took us a long time to realize that those products are never free and that what is expected in return costs more in terms of our time than if we were to purchase the items ourselves. A company once gave us a water maker with instructions from a professional on how to install it. It took us EIGHT DAYS to install! Similarly, Woody and Irenka were given a full complement of lithium batteries. When the batteries were delivered to Panama, Woody could not find an electrician who knew how to install them and had to teach himself how to do it. "It was a very steep learning curve," he says. In addition, their entire electrical system needed updating at a cost of a couple of thousand dollars. Sometimes, you're better off paying out of pocket for an item, rather than having to create the out of proportion amount of content demanded by the sponsor.

And remember that sponsorship comes in the form of 'stuff' rather than money into your pocket and, because it's hard to resist free stuff, you may end up with items on board that you don't actually need.

> **How to measure my online worth?**
>
> As with any other form of work, it is important that you understand the value of your time and know your worth per hour. If you have more than 100k subscribers, then I recommend that you find an agent to support you and negotiate with sponsors on your behalf. Social Bluebook (https://socialbluebook.com) is a great resource for content creators. It helps you to understand your worth, create a media kit, and it offers media training.

Tax and legalities

Irrespective of your work-while-cruising arrangements, it is important to consider the tax implications. Many countries will discontinue tax residency if you are out of the country for more than half the year. For Jessica and Jeroen, for example, officially emigrating from the Netherlands (to accommodate their sailing and to avoid the requirement that Benjamin and Frank be enrolled in formal education) means that Jessica will be deregistered from the country's list of freelancers and no longer be able to work as such in the Netherlands. She can, however, freelance via other countries. Although these options are more complicated, it is possible to acquire e-residency in countries such as Estonia or the Caymen Islands, while Spain has recently introduced a digital nomad law, with favorable conditions for digital work while resident in the country for less than half a year.

In addition to taxes, countries have different laws and regulations which may affect your ability to conduct your work. Do your research, and know your rights and obligations before you go.

Boat work, paid work, and kids

I know what you're thinking. It's all well and good keeping on top of your boat maintenance and earning a living while you go. But how on earth do you do that when you're also full-time parent, educator, and entertainer to your kids. If they're little, they need you so much of the time; if they're older, you've got home education to consider. Where do you find the time? And when do your actually get to enjoy cruising?

To be completely honest, we found it quite difficult with a new baby. But the one thing that kept us going (apart from loving what we do) was that we were determined to prove all those people wrong who said that as soon as we had a kid we could forget about sailing, forget about making videos, forget about our business. That gave us the motivation to feel as if we could accomplish everything!

The key to successfully carrying on working and sailing when Lenny was born was working as a team. One morning, Riley would put Lenny in the sling and go for long walks, giving me the space and time to edit and post videos, work on my social media accounts, catch up with collaborators, and so on. The next morning, we'd swap and I'd take Lenny while Riley got on with boat maintenance or planning our next passage. Of course, things went awry and it didn't always work out perfectly. But we were both very aware of how difficult it was for the other and, as much as we could, we gave each other space.

Sailing for so many years before having kids really prepared us. The boat was our home, sailing was our way of life. But it can be challenging no matter where you raise your kids, especially when you're trying to work full-time. After Darwin came along, we were better prepared, and we knew it wasn't going to be perfect. We knew that Riley or I (or both of us) could have two or more sleepless nights in a row and we'd still have to get up the next morning and work, from home, with two little kids. But there was no point in complaining or getting annoyed. It was what it was. We knew it was going to be tough at times and it was.

Sometimes, things got really bad – two crying, tired, grumpy little kids – and Riley and I would look at each other in empathy – I know, I know, this is shit, but this too shall pass. We were like robots in the early days – wake up, sail, film, do laptop work, do boat maintenance, all the while taking care of the babies and getting interrupted all day long. But we learned, if not to love the mess, then at least to accept it. It was the middle of COVID, so we knew how lucky we were to be able to work remotely and to be able to carry on doing what we loved.

So, full disclosure here, we hired a full-time nanny to help us out when Darwin was little. I know not everyone can do that. And not everyone would want to share their tiny home with someone else. But it worked for us. And that's the thing about cruising – make up your own rules to suit your family. Why try to be hard core when you don't need to be? Sailing and living aboard *La Vagabonde* is a full-time job for us and that was one area where we were happy to spend money to make money.

However, nanny or no nanny, here are some suggestions to make work onboard your boat manageable:

Establish clear roles

If you or your partner are engaged in regular ongoing work, then it is essential that you establish clear roles. Who is responsible for different aspects of child care, home education, grocery shopping, boat chores, etc.? Depending on the age of your kids, do they have roles too (chores, help with boat maintenance, education)? What space (head space and physical space) and time do you all need to accomplish those roles? If compromises need to be made, where and how will they be made? Juggling earning a living, maintaining your boat in good repair, and caring for (and educating) your kids are all highly time-consuming activities. By establishing clear roles, you ensure that none of these three aspects of your live aboard life are compromised. Also, when something unexpected happens, have a discussion about how this will affect your roles and what short- or long-term role changes need to be put in place.

Establish a routine

No matter how old your kids are, having an onboard routine makes life so much easier for everyone. Our routine has evolved over time in line with the boys' ages and abilities and it changes too depending on where we are and what we're doing. Our onboard daily routine, when we're not passage making, includes set times for breakfast, home schooling for Lenny, morning time off the boat, lunch together, afternoon family time on or off the boat, set supper and shower times for the boys, set bedtime. Having that routine makes work easier for both Riley and me, because all four of us know what to expect of each other at different times of the day.

Slow down

Back to this old nugget again, but it's really important when you're sailing with kids. If you try to quickly hop from place to place, pack in loads of cruising and exploring, then you're going to burn out. Jessica says that slowing down the pace of their lives has been to everyone's advantage. After the initial rush of sailing from the Netherlands to northern Spain, the family has learned to have "more time to not sail." With more time on their hands, she and Jeroen take turns to be with the children for long mornings, leaving the other free to work online, do boat maintenance, or have time for self-care. Forget about being in a rush to sail everywhere. Cruise at a pace that allows you to work *and* explore the places where you drop anchor.

Above: Lee, Taj, Bella and Sara *(Catalpa II)*

Below: Timmy, Ellen and Teddy *(Maes)*

Keeping the kids busy

While some might baulk at the idea of putting their little ones in front of a device to free up some time and space for work, the realities of living together 24/7 and finding time means that digital devices are sometimes necessary. Some sailing families have found that a less high-tech approach works very well. "We were in a marina," Martina recalls, "and an old man in a neighboring berth was doing a clear out of his boat. He offered us an old portable DVD player. We had a collection of DVDs onboard. That little DVD player didn't require a lot of power and it freed up my laptop, so that I could work while the girls watched a movie."

Jessica and Jeroen are also fans of the lowly DVD player. "We're just two parents," Jeroen says, "so it's nice sometimes to have your hands freed up." A low-tech DVD player has some advantages over a more high-tech device. It doesn't use any of your precious data budget and it allows for more parental control, as you have to manually insert a new disc, meaning your kids are less likely to watch endless programming (unless that's what you want them to do!).

Like other cruising families in this book, we've found it helpful for the boys to go to nursery or 'big' school when we've been in one place for a few weeks or months. We want the boys to meet local kids, to experience different ways of learning, to be immersed in a new culture. But it has the added bonus of freeing up our time, so we can both get jobs done in the few hours each day when they're off the boat. "It gave me a break that I needed," Irenka says of the months when her three kids went to school in Spain. "I got on with editing [YouTube content] for a few hours every morning."

Flexibility

Routines and roles are likely to change and it's important to remain flexible. There will be times when your established childcare and work rhythm simply will not work. "The rhythm is off for us right now," Jeroen said, as they prepared to cross the Atlantic. "I've got a lot of [boat repair and prep] chores to get done, so that's taking a toll on Jessica, who's spending more than her fair share of time with the boys. We'll get to a point where she needs to take more time off and, so long as we're honest with each other about that, it will be fine."

Tips

- Live simply and buy fresh food locally to keep household costs low

- Make the most of free activities such as hiking, museums and galleries, and free events such as local festivals

- A hybrid approach to cruising gives you the freedom to work and cruise at the same time or to alternate work and cruising time

- Content creation is a good option for some, but it takes a lot of dedicated work for it to pay off.

Chapter 9

Health and safety

Concern for your own and, even more so, your children's health while far out to sea or far from your home country is a concern for many parents who are considering cruising. These are valid concerns. But there are some simple steps you can take to ensure that everyone aboard is healthy and to enhance your ability to deal with small or major medical emergencies when they happen. In this chapter, I focus on caring for your physical and mental health, how to be as prepared as possible for emergencies, and staying safe at sea.

Self-care

One of the biggest challenges that cruising families face is being together 24/7. Jessica says, "You get less down time, less off time. That's something you have to learn to deal with. It's really hard if you're doing everything together all the time. You're making it really hard on yourself, trying to keep it fun for everyone. You have to remember to make time for your own well-being."

COVID-19 gave a lot of people an insight into what it's like to be at home with their loved ones all the time and the stress of being "up in each other's business," as Bella on *Catalpa* put it, juggling work and home education commitments. For Riley and me, giving each other space every day is a non-negotiable part of our relationship. From the moment the boys came along, no matter what was going on, we always made sure to give each other an hour or two in the day – to exercise, grab a coffee, write, meet other people. The kids might be screaming, the boat might be in chaos – it doesn't matter – it's time for one of us to take charge and give the other time for self-care.

I can't stress enough how important it is that you create time each day for self-care. When you are at anchor, or otherwise close to shore, the ideal situation is to get off the boat – go ashore for a walk or a run, take your tender/kayak/board for a paddle. For me, it's free diving. I return to the boat calm and relaxed, my batteries recharged. Sara says there are times when life on *Catalpa* just becomes too much; the kids are hungry, tired, and demanding, and Lee is driving her crazy. "I think, 'Are you kidding me? I need to get away from all of you just for a minute.'" Like me, Sara's go-to place is the water. "I need to jump off the boat and go underwater and I'm good. I come back out a new person. It's become an ongoing joke on the boat. If I'm losing it, the kids will say, 'Can you go jump in the water, please?' That's my coping mechanism." She says Bella and Taj now also take a dip in the sea when the rest of the family is simply too much for them.

Just because you live on a boat doesn't mean you have to give up your other hobbies and interests. Instead, give each other the time and space to indulge them. Despite being diving enthusiasts, Bart and Kim don't have a compressor on board. Sometimes, Kim will go away for an entire day of diving with a dive school, while Bart looks after Liz. Riley runs, Sara has yoga practice, Hazel engraves wood. Whatever your self-care hobby, make sure that you give yourself the time and space for it. And don't forget to give your kids the space to indulge in their hobbies too.

Of course, the ideal situation is to be left alone, either ashore or on the boat. But that's not always possible, for example, when on passage or when the weather conditions are poor. In those situations, it's still important to create space for each other. Creating 'me' time on a small boat can be a challenge, for sure. Even if you're

181

squirreled away in your cabin, you can still hear the sounds of crying/fighting/laughing going on in the rest of the boat. It's important that you discuss your need for self-care and that everyone sets clear boundaries and expectations for that self-care time. For parents with younger kids, self-care time for one parent means child-care time for the other. Let me stress – this cannot be child-care plus boat work/online work/chores/relaxing. The parent taking self-care time needs to know that they won't be disturbed because the other parent has decided it's a good time to multi-task. Listen to music or wear noise cancelling headphones to block out what's going on in the rest of the boat during your alone time. And make self-care part of your routine, so that your kids also become used to it and know that they have to respect when Mum or Dad are having alone time.

Being with your children 24/7 can be exhausting and can leave couples with little time for each other. It's easy to forget about each other when there is so much responsibility with children, a boat, and work. But you can't afford not to put your relationship with your partner front and center. Many sailing families find ingenious ways to have alone time, even when their children are very young. Jessica and Jeroen have a date night every Saturday evening. "We just take time for each other," Jeroen says. "We play a board game, watch a movie, or just talk." Very occasionally, another adult looks after Frank and Benjamin, such as their granddad when he comes to visit. "Otherwise, our date night is always on the boat," Jessica says. "The boys watch a DVD in their cabin and we have an hour or two that's just for us." Riley and I weren't nearly as organized, but we tried to make time for each other when Lenny napped during the day. Now that we have crew, it's easier. We stay on the boat while the crew take the boys off for a few hours, or we go off together and leave the boys onboard with our trusted crew.

Physical health

There aren't many modern lifestyles that are as healthy as cruising. Sailing keeps you physically fit and, in the absence of cars, cruising families tend to walk pretty much everywhere once we're ashore. However, there are some aspects of physical health that are important to consider.

Sun protection

Sailors spend a lot of time in the sun and we tend to be drawn to warmer climates. No matter where you cruise, it is essential that you protect your own skin and the delicate skin of your kids from UV radiation:

- Cover up: we wear hats, long-sleeved shirts, and sunglasses when out in the sun.

- Stay out of the middle of the day sun: given our lifestyle, we do this anyway. In a typical day, we go ashore in the morning, have lunch, nap, and relax in the middle of the day, and go out again in the evening, thus avoiding the sun when it's at its strongest.

- Limit sun exposure: we get no more than 30 minutes of skin exposure to the sun without sunscreen or clothing each day.

- Sunscreen: we use mineral-based reef safe 50SPF.[13] It's hard to find the good stuff once you set sail; stock up before you begin your voyage or take advantage of a Westernized supermarket or pharmacy when you find one and stock up. Our rule for kids and adults alike

---

13   Many sailors, including us, make their own sunscreen. Here's a recipe that we've used in the past: https://iquitplastics.com/blog/reef-safe-sunscreen-recipe?format=amp

is that we put sunscreen on our faces and necks when
we emerge from our cabins in the morning.

Childhood immunization

Every country has a slightly different childhood immunization
schedule. For instance, the MMR[14] first dose is given to babies at
roughly the same age in the US and the UK, but the second dose is
given to children in the UK at 3–5 years (or earlier) and in the US
at 4–6 years; while the fourth dose of DTaP[15] is, in some countries,
dependent on the age at which children are expected to start school.
These may not seem like major differences, but if you want to stick
to the immunization schedule that your child started on, you'll need
proof of that schedule and evidence of the immunizations they've
already had.

Because Lenny and Darwin were born in Australia, we stick
to the Australian schedule. As in many countries, they each received
medical record books with immunization cards when they were
born. It's a really good book to have. If you don't have a book, then
I recommend you ask your GP for an official printout of your kid's
immunization record. Martina's daughters are 13 and 14 years old
now and have had their childhood immunizations in three different
countries. "When it was time for their next shot, I simply showed the
book to a nurse in a health center, showing when they had their last
shots and the schedule that I wanted them to follow. I've never had
any problems doing that."

My boys have had their shots everywhere too – Australia, the
US, the Bahamas, Portugal. Who knows where we'll be when it's
time for their next shots. Finding a pediatrician, clinic, health center,
or GP in a new country can sometimes be a challenge. A Google

---

14   MMR: Measles, mumps, and rubella.
15   DTaP: Diphtheria, tetanus, acellular pertussis (whooping cough).

Darry and Yewan *(Mothership)*

search will sometimes point you in the right direction. I also suggest getting information about health services from the local town hall where you're at anchor.

Some forward planning might be in order if your kid is due a multi-part immunization. In the past, we've found a nice location and stayed put for a few weeks or even months to accommodate one of the boys having a multi-part immunization with weeks between each shot. We've also delayed a couple of shots by a few months until a time that suited us better.

Finally, a few of things to bear in mind. First, if you don't have health insurance for the US, getting childhood immunizations there can be very expensive. We spent a lot of time in the Bahamas when the boys were younger, where they have all the same services, but at a half or a quarter of the price in the US. Second, in smaller and more out of the way places, it is important to plan ahead. Clinics may not have a particular shot on hand, and ordering it in may take a few days. So, plan immunizations in advance and give the clinic plenty of time. Finally, day care, kindergartens, and primary schools in a lot of countries will not allow children to enroll without proof of up-to-date immunization. Therefore, if you intend to enroll your kid in formal care or education during or after your time cruising, then make sure you keep up with your immunization schedule.

Regular checkups

Before the kids came along, Riley and I flew back to Australia once a year to visit family and friends, and we'd schedule annual health and dental check-ups, making sure we were in tip-top condition before we returned to the boat. However, once the boys came along, those annual trips dried up. That was partly because we now felt that we were our own family with our own place (i.e., *La Vagabonde II*) and partly because long-haul travel with two small kids is exhausting and expensive. So, we stopped having those annual check-ups in our home country. Undoubtedly, this has made regular check-ups for us and for the boys more difficult. We can no longer make an appointment at a clinic that has all our records to hand, where we have all the associated benefits of being a citizen of that country, and where we speak the language and understand the culture of healthcare.

But that hasn't put us off. It simply means that we have to do some advance research. In the US (where everything is super expensive if you don't have health insurance), kids usually visit a pediatrician; however, in many other countries, you can just take your kid to the regular GP for check-ups. That way, all the family can be checked by the same medical professional. When we want to schedule check-ups, we always start with a Google search of what healthcare services are available in the area we are in or plan to be in. As with the immunizations, we'll visit local town halls to ask about medical services in the area. In many places, due to language barriers (even if people speak the same language as you, accents and local dialects may vary), we find it easier to visit the clinic to speak to someone at the front desk, rather than try to explain our situation and make appointments over the phone. Explaining that we've arrived by boat, that we don't have a GP back in our home country, that we don't live in our home country – or, indeed, in any country – can be hard at the best of times. Doing it face-to-face makes it a little easier to comprehend.

Having the correct documents to hand will make your entry into a new healthcare system much easier. If you are visiting a clinic to make an appointment for the first time, make sure to take the baby book/immunization card that I mentioned in the previous section, together with all your passports, proof of medical insurance (if you have it), and your kid's birth certificate, especially if you have different surnames. This will smooth your entry into the system.

Remember to be patient, especially if you are using public health services. You and your family are an addition to what, in pretty much every country in the world, is an overburdened system. Be prepared for long waiting times, for busy waiting rooms, and for you to be deprioritized. Staff will do their best to see everyone in a timely manner on limited resources.

Medical insurance

Good medical insurance cover will give you the peace of mind that, if anything goes wrong, you won't face insurmountable medical bills. In some places, in the case of non-life-threatening medical emergencies, you will not be treated without first proving that you have medical insurance. *La Vagabonde III* is covered by Pantanious Insurance which provides cover both for the boat and for the people on the boat. It covers any personal accidents that occur on the boat or 24 hours of being on the boat (e.g., our medical costs would be covered if we were to go ashore and have an accident off a hired scooter). Because we often spend a couple of weeks or more off the boat, we also have general travel insurance. Some cruising families choose not to get either boat insurance or personal insurance. We wouldn't sail without either, for the peace of mind they give us.

Luckily, we've had no major medical emergencies. For smaller emergencies, we've generally found it easier to pay the bill ourselves to avoid the hours of headache inducing paperwork and emails needed to make the claim.

Medical emergencies

You are human. You have kids. There will be medical emergencies. No matter where or how you live in the world, shit happens, so be prepared to deal with it. It's often the thing that non-live aboards or not-yet-liveaboard are most concerned with: What to do if someone breaks a bone/gets appendicitis/bangs their head when you're in the middle of the ocean. Let me tell you, these things, and worse, have happened to people at sea. Most have survived. Some haven't. But you could say the same about pretty much anything in life. Being close to a hospital doesn't mean that someone will survive a medical emergency. The best you can do is be prepared. And when a medical emergency presents itself, have the skills and the resources to hand to deal with it.

We've had a few crises over the years. We've had three midnight visits to the emergency room because of Lenny's breathing difficulties due to croup, which can be life threatening. Each time it happened, we were in a marina or at anchor, and close to a hospital. In addition, he sometimes struggles to breathe when he has a respiratory virus. He also choked on a piece of melon once when we were on land. And, of course, there's his nut allergy (see below). Before the boys were born, I contracted ciguatera from eating an infected trevally that we had caught trawling. We were anchored in rough seas off Saba, in the Lesser Antilles. I woke up with vomiting and diarrhea, feeling dizzy and weak, and unable to stand up. My senses were all messed up – cold things felt hot – and my lips were tingling. Riley had to get me into the dinghy and across some pretty big waves to shore. He then hailed down a truck, and the guy brought us to the hospital which was on top of a mountainous volcanic island, that reached the clouds. It was pretty scary. You simply don't know what's going to happen to you or your kids. But there are some steps you can take to be as prepared as possible.

Medical kit

Before you set sail, make sure you have a well-stocked first aid kit. While you can buy first aid and medical kits for ocean passages or for cruising in general, most don't have families in mind and are often geared toward older cruisers. If you buy a standard one, you're likely to end up with unnecessary items, such as heart medicines, but not enough of what you actually need, such as medical glue and Steri-strips, which are the two most commonly used items in our first aid kit, because, kids being kids, the boys are always busting open their knees, elbows, foreheads, chins.

You can put together your own bespoke first aid/medical kit, based on expert advice. Since the boys were born, we have always sought the assistance of their pediatrician. We have explained our cruising plans and the pediatrician has written as many prescriptions as they can for the most likely accidents and medical emergencies. I am always surprised by just how many prescriptions they've been able to give us. You can do the same with your own doctor, and thus have a well-stocked medical cabinet for all on board.

However, the problem with this method is that many medicines expire after six months. When you're overseas, which cruisers tend to be, it can be difficult to convince a doctor who's meeting you for the first time to give you prescriptions for all the medicines you're requesting. Doctors have turned down our request for prescriptions in the past because they simply don't understand our situation. But we've discovered a great trick to get around this problem, which I wish I'd known about sooner: find a doctor who is also a sailor. You can do this by posting on Facebook pages or other online resources for sailors or cruisers in whatever area of the world you're in, stating that you are seeking a doctor who will understand the situation. We have done this a few times and it's made it so much easier to get the prescriptions we need to top up our medical kit.

An alternative, but more expensive, option is to buy a medical kit from a company such as Medical Support Offshore (MSOS, see Resources), which creates bespoke kits based on the ages of the people on board, the types of activities you're likely to engage in (e.g., diving, hiking, etc.), and the type of sailing you're doing (e.g., inshore day sailing or ocean crossings). MSOS also creates bespoke grab bags in case you have to abandon ship in an emergency situation, and provides a range of supporting services, that I'll tell you about below.

Emergency Medical Training

Before you untie from the dock and take your kids out to sea, get some emergency training under your belt. It could save someone's life someday. A few years ago, Riley and I completed the MSOS proficiency in medical first aid course. It was a three and a half-day course with an instructor who had three decades of wilderness survival training. We were put through our paces and it certainly gave us peace of mind. All the families who contributed to this book have some sort of emergency training or other. Irenka and Woody had sea-specific emergency training for their jobs as sailing instructors before they set sail on *Mothership*, Bart is a nurse and Jeroen completed three years of a nursing degree, Julian achieved medical care proficiency in preparation for deep field research in Antarctica, and Martina did a three-day pediatric first aid course. In other words, there are many ways to get first aid and medical emergency training. I strongly recommend that both adults have at least some emergency training, and if you can do a course that is bespoke to your family and your cruising plans, then all the better.

Our MSOS course was not very expensive, and it's worth its weight in gold in the peace of mind it has given us knowing that we should be able to act quickly in most medical emergencies.

However, Jeroen says, "Even though I've been in emergency situations, they've never been with my own children. I don't know if I'd be as professional as I was when I was in a hospital situation and it was my job." Jessica says, "But if there's no backup, you just have to get your shit together. Don't panic. Keep your shit together and fix the problem. Because there's no doctor you can call."

You could go years and not have to use your medical or first aid training and your skills can quickly become rusty. We do a refresher course every couple of years. If that's not possible, there are plenty of valuable videos on YouTube that you can watch as a refresher. Make sure to choose videos that are endorsed and/or created by a reputable organization or institution. In addition, set yourself a reminder to go through your medical kit every few months. See what's in there, remove anything that's out of date and take note of what needs to be replaced. While you're doing that, practice stitching a wound, drawing liquid into a needle, and so on, just to keep your skills sharp. If you don't practice it, you'll forget.

Emergency scenarios

In addition to getting certified in advanced first aid and emergency response, envisaging what emergency situations you might face can really prepare you for what to do if something happens. Riley and I have worked out five realistic emergency scenarios that we might face. These five are: (1) broken limb or impact wound; (2) venomous bite or sting; (3) Riley injuring his neck again; (4) Lenny having a severe allergic reaction; and (5) man overboard. At each new place we visit, we talk through what we would do if one of those scenarios were to happen. Each place is different and knowing what challenges we would face in an emergency situation can help us to better prepare for it. For instance, it's not uncommon for us to anchor in locations that are two days from the nearest hospital. In the Bahamas, where we spent a lot of time when the boys were younger, our options in a serious emergency might be to charter a private plane or a speed boat. Both are expensive options, and it could still be six hours before we reached a hospital. I certainly don't want to put anyone off cruising in more remote waters. Far from it. Rather, be prepared. If you know that you'll be somewhere remote, work out possible scenarios, what order do you need to make things happen, and how much will you have to depend on your own knowledge and skills in a given situation.

- Familiarize yourself with each new area. You can make this part of your morning run, your trip to the market or the playground. Take note of the location of clinics, pharmacies, hospitals, emergency services, and other important buildings such as the police station or town hall. If you are in a smaller community, check local opening hours and what you would have to do if you needed medical care out of hours.

- Write down the local emergency services and other important phone numbers and keep them somewhere obvious, such as above the navigation table. You don't want to have to search for a phone number once you're in the middle of the emergency. Pilot books and almanacs generally have this information, but beware: it may not be up to date. When you go ashore, check with an official source (police, town hall, harbor master) if those numbers are correct.

- Know the best way to make contact in an emergency. In some parts of the world, for example, you're more likely to make contact with the harbor by mobile phone than over VHF.

- How far is it to the nearest doctor, health centre, hospital, and what is your plan to get there in an emergency? Are there water taxis, high speed boats, planes, etc., that can come to your aid at short notice? And how can you get in touch with those services?

For the vast majority of cruisers, such emergencies will never occur. But every one of us should be prepared in case they happen to us.

Professional support

It is increasingly possible to have digital professional support in the event of an emergency. MSOS, in addition to training and medical kits, provides round-the-clock telemedical care to its members and can be accessed by satellite phone or Starlink. It offers different membership packages and knowing we have that telehealth support if we need it makes me feel a lot more comfortable about sailing out into the ocean for days or weeks at a time.

Depending on your private or public medical insurance, you may also have access to 24/7 emergency telehealth care. Jessic and Jeroen, for example, can avail of free-to-use 24-hour emergency care from doctors in the Netherlands who can provide advice and guidance over their satellite phone using the 100 free phone minutes per month they have with their Iridium Go contract. "We save those minutes up," Jessica said. "On the last day of the month, if we haven't used them, we call our family and friends."

Documentation

To make accessing emergency medical care as simple as possible, make sure that you have copies of all your important documents with you. Rather than carrying the originals around, Riley and I each have a photo album on our phones containing images of all our passports, health insurance documents, and any other documents that we might have to show. A health service might still want to see the originals, but the copy on the phone will get you in the door.

Martina's daughter Lily fell and banged her head while at a playground in a village in Spain. She was showing signs of concussion – double vision, drowsiness, and vomiting. It was out of hours for the local health center and so Martina found a friendly ex-pat who drove her and Lily to a 24-hour health centre 25km away. The doctor on call suspected concussion and sent Lily to A&E at a hospital a further 50km away. Despite the referral letter from the doctor, Martina struggled to have Lily admitted, because she didn't have any documentation to hand. Both of their passports and their European health cards were aboard *Carina*, 75km away. Due to poor phone coverage at their anchorage, Martina failed to get in touch with Julian, who she hoped would be able to send photos of the passports and health cards. Lily was eventually admitted, but not before Martina shed a few tears. "Once we got past the dragon on the front desk, all the medical staff were so kind to us. But I learned my lesson to never leave home without at least a copy of our passports, health cards, and other important documents on our phones."

Food allergies and intolerances

We sailed non-stop for 19 days from the US to Portugal when Lenny was one year old. Little did we know that he was on the cusp of developing a potentially life-threatening allergy to nuts. He ate peanut butter and peanut products on that trip with no reaction. We made land at Lisbon and then flew to Australia for Christmas. The next time he ate peanut butter he had an anaphylactic reaction. His lips and throat swelled up; he couldn't breathe. It's too scary to think of what might have happened if he'd had this reaction while we were at sea. A standard prick test revealed that, in addition to peanuts, he's allergic to tree nuts (almonds, Brazil nuts, cashews, hazelnuts, pecans, pistachios, walnuts), sesame seeds, kiwi fruit, and dust mites.

After we got over the initial shock of Lenny having these allergies, it felt like we could do anything. Those allergies weren't going to hold him or us back. We've made some adjustments to prevent Lenny from accidentally consuming any of the products he's allergic to:

- In general, we don't buy any products that contain those ingredients

- We have a 'no waste' rule, so if someone accidentally buys, for example, almond milk, we write 'No Lenny' in permanent marker on it

- We've been in southeast Asia for the past couple of years, where food is commonly cooked in peanut oil or sesame oil and sesame seeds are sprinkled over everything Therefore, the food we eat ashore is very basic – plain rice, steamed vegetables

- We always ask about ingredients in restaurants. Most restaurants are happy to accommodate

- We carry epi pens on board and have one with us at all times when we go ashore. They require a prescription. The first doctor I asked, refused to prescribe them and I had to go elsewhere.

Ours aren't the only children with allergies or intolerances. Five-year-old Benjamin on *Sans Souci* has a gluten intolerance. His parents have found this intolerance easier to adapt to in some countries than others. Southern European countries, for example, have much clearer gluten labelling than their home country of the Netherlands, and restaurant staff are much more aware of which menu items contain gluten and which don't. For their Atlantic crossing, the family carried a supply of gluten free flours to bake their own bread. "But there are always gluten-free options," Jessica says, adding that they intend to change their diet when they reach the Caribbean, to match what's available locally. "We're not going to provision for five years!" she says.

If your child has an allergy or an intolerance:

- Keep a supply of suitable long-life foods on board

- Undertake research prior to travelling to a new country or region to learn about local cuisine, availability of suitable foods for your child, and allergy labelling and awareness

- Within the limits of your child's allergy or intolerance, adapt to local diets and cuisines.

- Every boat have adult and child epi-pens in stock, even if no-one aboard has allergies.

Safety at sea
Seasickness

In Chapter 2, I mentioned seasickness in the context of pregnancy. Here I want to explore it more broadly. If you've ever felt seasick, you'll know that it's no fun. It can be extremely debilitating, and even dangerous at its most extreme. Having a child who regularly gets seasick is likely to make you reconsider your entire cruising plan. However, you'll be pleased to know that most people adjust and their seasickness abates over time. There are also some steps you can take to reduce the chances of feeling seasick in the first place.

When Jessica and Jeroen first set sail, Benjamin experienced seasickness for some time. His parents tried different approaches. "Those anti-seasickness bracelets didn't work and the kids complained that they were uncomfortable to wear." In Spain, they bought an anti-seasickness medicated drink. "That was horrible because he got really drowsy. Even when there were dolphins around the boat, he was falling asleep." In the end, Jessica and Jeroen realized that the best way to avert seasickness was to distract Benjamin. "He watches something on the iPad," Jessica says. "I don't know how. If I did that, it would make me feel even worse. But putting on Paw Patrol works for him. And then he wants to eat." These days, if he starts to feel unwell, he goes to his parent's bed and sleeps for two or three hours. "When he wakes up, he feels fine," his dad says.

"At first, we were really worried," Jeroen says. "We thought, 'What are we doing to our kids?' But then we thought that if they were in daycare or in school, there would be occasional times when they would be sick too. All kids get sick now and again. For our son, it's occasional bouts of seasickness when we're passage making. And he doesn't get colds and flus that kids in school get. That put it into perspective for us."

It took almost a season of cruising for Martina and Julian to recognize the pattern that caused one-year-old Katie's seasickness. Katie would take her afternoon nap in a saloon berth, where her parents could keep an eye on her from the cockpit. "I usually let her wake gradually from her nap, give her time to come round and wake up fully before I'd take her up to join us in the cockpit." That led to spectacular vomiting sessions – across the saloon, from the companionway up into the cockpit, all over Martina. "I was stupidly slow at reading the signs," Martina laughs. "If I whipped her up out of bed and up into the cockpit as soon as she woke up, then she wouldn't vomit. But leaving her below deck, even for ten minutes, was asking for trouble." Once the trigger for Katie's vomiting was established, she never did it again.

Watch for triggers. Some people (adults and children) are more prone to seasickness if they are cold, have a full bladder, are hungry, or are thirsty. Putting your head down to read is a trigger for many people, but is curiously comforting for others. Your children often can't explain what is making them feel bad, so you'll have to learn to read the signs.

Man overboard

Do you know what you would do if one of your children fell overboard while you're underway? Or what you or your partner would do if either of you fell overboard? Have you discussed it with your partner? Stop what you're doing right now and have that discussion. Have that discussion in the cockpit of your boat, where you can see where everything is, what obstacles will be in your way, where the nearest life ring is and how easy it will be for you to grab it. Discuss which one of you is better at maneuvering the boat in a man overboard situation. If you've got more than one kid, discuss various scenarios of where the other kid might be or what they might be doing while you're dealing with your MOB situation.

Our plan, if one of our boys goes in the water with a lifejacket on, is that I will grab the life ring and jump in the water. Why me? Riley's faster at getting the sails down. I'll swim to the kid and then hold on to him and the life ring, while Riley turns the boat around and comes back for us. With the life jacket on, the kid's going to float and I can swim, so it's a matter of holding on and waiting for Riley to come get us. Same goes for a kid falling in without a life jacket. It's just way more urgent and critical. Our plan might not be the best one and your plan could well be different. But it's something you should think about.

When all's said and done, if you child falls in, you have to make the split-second decision to grab a floatation device (life ring) before you jump in or to jump in without it. Will the instinct to jump in to save your baby overcome your ability to take the logical course of action and stop for the extra second to grab the life ring? We have a life ring on one side of the boat at the back and a U-sling on the other. The life ring isn't attached to the boat, but the U-sling is, on a long tether. Which will I go for?

Just as I recommended practicing your first aid and emergency medical procedures, it's important that you practice your MOB moves. You can do this while you are underway by throwing something overboard and then going through the process of dropping the sails, turning the boat around, heaving to, and retrieving the item from the water. Review your procedure afterwards – what worked, what do you still need to improve on? Timmy once threw his toy cat over the side to be rescued, but seagulls immediately pounced on it and the man overboard became a different sort of rescue mission. As Timmy cried for his set upon toy, Carola and Teddy lined up and managed to throw a net over the cat to pull it back in. "Those seagulls were really nasty because they pulled its eyes out," Carola said.

However, as Jessica points out, "The chance that you'll be saved is slim anyway. The primary thing is to not fall overboard in the first place." Which brings us back to the question of lifejackets, tethers, and where on deck your children are allowed to be. At sea, we have a rule that the boys are only allowed in the cockpit and only if one of us is there. Before they step outside the saloon door, they must have their life jackets on. Martina eschewed bulky life jackets

Safety net *(Tranquillity)*

in the cockpit in favor of harnesses and straps. "As soon as they came out of the saloon, it was second nature to them to hook onto the cockpit rings. They wore web harnesses on their torsos, with quick release straps. The straps were long enough that they could easily move around our small cockpit, play with their toys, kneel or stand up to look over the side of the deep center cockpit. And, if we were lucky enough to have dolphins on our bow, we put their life jackets on and hooked their safety harnesses onto the jackstays so they could walk the length of the boat to see our visitors.

It is advised that adults in the cockpit alone and/or after dark should wear both a life jacket and be tethered to the boat. Aboard *Ros Ailither*, the whole family wore life jackets on deck all the time, once Katie and Reuben complained that it was unfair that they had to wear life jackets, while their parents didn't. "We never had a plan for what we would do if one of them fell in," Hazel says. "Rather, we tried to minimize the possibility of anyone going overboard."

Abandoning ship

In addition to five emergency scenarios I mentioned above, you should also have a plan of action for abandoning ship. There are lots of resources out there with advice about abandoning ship into your life raft, so I won't rehash these here. However, work out with your partner what roles you would both play with regard to getting your children from the boat to the lifeboat, what your backup plan would be if one of you was incapacitated, and so on. Hazel says, "I worried about how we would get the baby into a life raft if we had to abandon ship. Would it be better to put her in a life jacket and then tie her to me? What if the rope got tangled in something? There are all sorts of worries. In the end, I decided I had to stop worrying, because if I worried too much, my milk would dry up and then I'd have a more serious problem on my hands."

Make sure that your life raft and life jackets are regularly serviced. Have fire extinguishers throughout the boat and gas cutoff valves. Be vigilant, be careful. Slow down and make sure to get enough sleep. These will help to prevent accidents or reduce their severity.

Tips

- Living with your entire family in close quarters all day every day can be difficult. Create time and space for everyone's self-care

- Ensure the ease and efficiency of regular childhood health care by keeping a record of your child's inoculations and check-ups, and having copies of other identification and insurance documents

- Create a bespoke medical kit that matches the profiles of those on your boat

- Get advanced first aid or medical care training and keep your skills up-to-date

- Discuss different emergency scenarios and how you would deal with them in different geographical settings

Chapter 10

Do it your way

If I have sought to do anything in these pages, it has been to inspire you to put your dream into action. I wanted to give you the confidence to sail with your family *in your own way*. There is no right or wrong way to live aboard a boat with your kids. There's no ideal family, no ideal boat, no ideal way of cruising. The seven families and I, through our years of experience, have worked out, through trial and error, what works for us. We hope that some of our insights will be adaptable to your family's cruising life. In this final chapter, I will explore the pros and cons of taking on crew to help make those big passages a bit easier, and I will look beyond live aboard life, to how to prepare to move your family ashore once again.

Crew

Even before I met Riley, he often had friends and family members fly up from Australia to the Mediterranean for a few weeks at a time, to crew for him on various legs of his cruise and to help him with maintenance and repair jobs. We carried on in that way until 2018, when we got our first official crew member aboard. We haven't looked back.

Don't be afraid to consider crew. A lot of families take on crew, particularly for longer passages, such as ocean crossings. Many will come aboard for free in return for the trip. You can find crew in all sorts of places. We've been lucky enough to meet people along the way or, because of our social media profile, people have contacted us to ask if they can crew for us. There are various crewing websites that people have successfully used to find a match. And there are places in the world, such as the Canary Islands in late autumn and early winter, where prospective crew hang out, hoping to be picked up for an Atlantic crossing. It doesn't really matter where you find your crew, so long as you follow some golden rules when vetting them.

Getting people on board to help us out was the best thing we did. We've had some great crew over the years. Women and men who really know their way around a boat, who can anticipate what the skipper needs before he even knows it himself. Who are open and willing to learn. Who are good company and who cheerfully share our manic space in a whirlwind of two energetic little boys, at risk of being filmed for our YouTube channel at any time of the day, with a sometimes grumpy skipper, and a sometimes overwrought skipper's mate. They make themselves at home, while also knowing how to give us our family space.

But we've also had some not-so-great crew over the years. That was generally down to our own naivete. Back in the early days, before the kids came along, we often took crew on board who wanted to get from A to B and who assured us that they had sailing experience. Foolishly, we didn't ask for references or proof, and some of them turned out to have no sailing experience at all. Not only were they completely unhelpful, we ended up having to care for them and they were simply another mouth to feed. We couldn't even trust them to keep watch, given how little experience they had. Woody and Irenka also made the mistake of taking on crew with no prior sailing experience. "We found this woman at the yacht club. She'd never been sailing before, but it was her dream. She came on board to help with the kids and was badly seasick for the entire passage. We ended up looking after the kids AND her."

These days, we have golden rules for choosing crew. I want to know the following:

- Proof of how many miles of sailing they already have under their belt. I want someone with some experience.

- References from people they've crewed for or sailed with. This is especially important if you are getting crew for free. Many people want to crew as an adventure, as a way to travel and see the world. That's great for them. But not great for you if you end up with some useless extra body on board, when what you really need is an extra pair of hands, eyes, feet.

- Because we sail with our two young children, we also look for police clearance or similar.

Over the years, we have had different types of crew – to help with sailing, to look after the children, to help with filming. The first thing I look for in someone who will have responsibility for the children is willingness to listen. How well do they pay attention to conversations or to instructions. Some people simply don't listen to instructions, and there's no time for that aboard a boat with small children. I also want to know how quickly they react to situations, because sometimes you only have a split second to grab a child's arm or catch a pot if it decides to fly across the saloon in sudden bad weather. They need to be very alert.

Of course, it also helps that the boys like the crew. Lenny is very confident and independent, so he needs an adult who can show him direction and be firm. In the past, we've had the occasional crew member who was a little too nice to Lenny and he walked all over them. That's super unhelpful for Riley and me. I realize that it's a tricky situation to come into someone else's very small home, and to be tasked with caring for two kids while their parents are right there, in the same space. I can see how that might be intimidating for prospective crew. But, at heart, we're always looking for a combination of firmness and kindness.

As I mentioned in Chapter 2, give some consideration to the emotional as well as the practical reasons for having crew on board. In a family in which I am definitely in the minority, it's nice to have some female energy around.

Sometimes, your prospective crew can have criteria for choosing you. Valentin and Juliana had no sailing experience when they started out, and found crew on the *Boatfinder* website to help them with various stages of their passage from the Mediterranean to the Baltic Sea and back again. Valentin and Arvin were sailing across the Bay of Biscay, while Juliana took the other three boys back to Germany for school. "We found this skipper from Switzerland who sent me a list of the things he expected on the boat, do to with safety, charts, and so on. He asked how many people would be on board. When I told him just me and my 13-year-old son, he said, 'That's not enough.' Two hours later he called back to say he had five more people. He's in a WhatsApp group of sailors, and he posted the passage and the dates and asked if anyone wanted to do it to gain the miles for their Offshore Yachtmaster qualification." For Valentin, this was good news. Rather than day sailors who wanted to hop from port to port, the crew consisted of a bunch of experienced sailors who wanted to make as much ground as possible in as little time as possible. "We sailed with that crew from Porto in Portugal to Cherbourg in France – 700 NM. The Swiss guy taught me how to use a sextant, how to seriously navigate with charts, how to take compass bearings at night. It was very instructive."

Once your crew are onboard, it's important to set down ground rules, irrespective of whether they are family or friends or crew you've never met before. Woody and Irenka learned this the hard way. "We didn't really have any rules for people at the start. Friends arrived to crew for us. We were at the supermarket and one

205

of them was adding extra crates of beer to our shopping, while we were thinking 'this isn't really what we need for a four-day passage.'"

Clearly set out in writing the tasks you want your crew to perform, which of you will be their skipper/boss (this depends on what you've brought them on for), and the hours they will be expected to crew. In addition, make it clear if they will be expected to contribute to cooking, cleaning, and so on. If so, how and when? Make them aware of things that are not allowed on your boat (smoking, drug taking) or not allowed while they are performing their crewing duties. Have all these ground rules in writing so there is no room for confusion.

Moving ashore

There are all sorts of reasons why people move ashore again and sometimes the transition from sea to land can be a bit bumpy. For some, the transition back to land is organic, for others it's always been part of the cruising plan, and for others still, it can come about following a lot of soul searching or because someone on board is not happy with cruising life.

Organic move

Martina and Julian never intended to move ashore. They were en route to northern Spain from the Mediterranean when they decided to check out a river that lots of other sailors had recommended to them. "It was beautiful up the river," Martina recalls. "So peaceful, the only sound when we cut the engine was sheep bells." A Spanish family anchored next to them told them great things about the tiny village school where they had temporarily enrolled their sons. Lots of yachtie kids went to the little three-teacher school and the teachers were used to international kids dropping in for a term or two. Fully committed to home educating Lily and Katie, Martina and Julian decided to enroll them in the school for a term to immerse them in

Above: *Argo* family
Below: *Sans Souci* family

Spanish language and culture. That was nine years ago, and they've been in the village ever since. They continued living on the boat, with each passing school term saying 'Just one more term.' At the same time, Martina's freelance business was growing, she needed space to work, and their 36ft Westerly Conway was beginning to feel decidedly small. After three years at anchor in the river or tied alongside the village pontoon, they decided to move ashore. "The move ashore itself was very organic," Martina says, "but I was very emotional about it because it meant the end of the sailing dream. Even though I had chosen this village and to move ashore, it took me a long time to realize that the end of the sailing dream wasn't a bad thing. It had just been replaced by something just as special."

It's ok to change your mind. Most of us set out with a dream and with a plan in mind. We're going to cross the Atlantic or the Pacific. We're going to circumnavigate. We're going to sail from the UK to Greece, or from Australia to Alaska. Whatever. But sometimes those plans change. And sometimes the dream changes. And that's ok. That's perfectly ok. Riley and I have realized in the past few years that we want a more hybrid lifestyle. The idea of spending most of our time on the boat no longer appeals as much as it once did. The boat is our home and we love sailing her. But we want to have more adventures ashore, to rent properties for a few months at a time and really immerse ourselves in places and cultures. It's the next step in our family's evolution.

Adapting to a new life

Hazel says moving ashore has taken a lot of getting used to. She admits the family doesn't feel as close as it used to. "On a boat, you always see where everyone else is, but ashore, they just disappear into different corners of the house. I miss the closeness of everybody, when we were all in the same space together. We've lost the togetherness." She also thinks they've got a bit lazy. When they were on the boat, they'd look out and see that it was a beautiful day. "Someone would say, 'Let's go out in the kayaks' and we'd just do it. But now, if we think we'd like to do that, we have to check the tides, check the weather. We're definitely not as spontaneous any more. It's only a five-minute bike ride to the river, but we just don't get out on it as much."

On the other hand, she enjoys the space of being in a house and of having a garden to tend. As the children grow older and become more independent, being on land means they can come and go with greater freedom. Friends can come to visit without having to be picked up in the dinghy. "It's also easier," Hazel said. "You don't have to keep searching for petrol stations and figuring out how to get to them to fill the dinghy motor. You don't have to keep going ashore to get water."

A plan realized

The crew of *Mothership* are over halfway through their circum-navigation and have started to think about what they'll do when they get back to the UK. "The circumnavigation was the main goal," Irenka says. "The rough plan is to sell the boat, think about the kids' exams, and work out what we're going to do when we get back. The boat is a good circumnavigator, but we don't need this size boat if we're going to stay in Europe." Irenka admits that, at the back of her mind, she thought the family might have found "some deserted island" and stayed there. "That was a kind of fantasy," she says. "There are so many places where people stop, but I've not found a place yet where I'd want to stop." Woody, however, says, "Martinique, French Polynesia, places like that. It's difficult to push yourself on."

The circumnavigation has helped Irenka realize the importance of community. "When you leave a place where you've made friends, you realize how important those people are," she says. "It's taken me till this far, half way around the world, to realize how important community and friends are. We have that community back in the UK."

The transition for children

Children often have mixed feelings about moving ashore and the realities of formal education following years of home schooling can come as a shock. Rowan has had to adjust to different social rules at her school in the UK. Used to befriending every kid she met when she was sailing, it took her some time to realize that school was just too big to be friends with everyone. "It's quite nice actually," she says, "you can be a bit more picky and choosy." She has found the texture of friendships quite different too. "Girls talk about each other behind their backs," she says. "You see it in movies, but I didn't realize it actually happens." Boat kids, used to being in the company of people of all ages, also wonder at the more distant relationships between adults and children, in which most adults outside the family circle are only known as rather vague authority figures, such as teachers.

Darry and Yewan have mixed feelings about returning to England. While Yewen will be happy to return to formal education, to meet up with his old friends again, he says he'll be sad to leave the boat and the experiences he's had. "When I'm older, I'm definitely going to have lots of holidays and visit the places I liked the most on this trip," he says.

Do it your way

I wouldn't change the life we've chosen for anything. My little family lives a magical life. But it's not a fantasy life. Like any life, it has its ups and downs, its stresses and strains. But it's a life lived according to our own rules, immersed in nature, watching our beautiful boys grow. I see how healthy they are, the great variety of people they meet, the fun they have. Who wouldn't want this life for their kids?

To anyone who's considering this transition, Hazel says, "Definitely do it. You're not going to regret it. Even if the children don't remember it all, you'll have the memories and they'll be learning all the time. Living on a boat, you're more connected to nature, you're part of the big wide world. There's no experience in the world like sitting in the bow and looking down at dolphins at the front of the boat. Or seeing a jellyfish go by. You don't have to go anywhere to see wildlife. It's just there."

"We could have been financially smarter and bought a better boat," Sara says. "But then, we could still be saving money and preparing and the moment would have passed. We might never have left. I'm glad we did it when we did."

Irenka says, "We put all this energy into our family and now we're enjoying it, having all these amazing adventures, meeting amazing people. Despite all the things that make it difficult, the fact that we're doing this thing together as a family is the best thing."

So, what are you waiting for?

Tips

- Make sure your crew have prior experience and come with good references
- It's ok to change your mind
- The transition back to land and to school may be bumpy for all members of the family

Resources

Social media of contributing families
San Souci
Instagram: @Sanssoucisailing
@Jess_watalsjedeloterijnietwint
YouTube: https://www.youtube.com/@Watalsjedeloterijnietwint

Mothership
Instagram: @mothershipadrift
YouTube: https://www.youtube.com/@MotherShipAdrift
Website: https://www.mothershipadrift.com

Catalpa II
Instagram: @sailingcatalpa @artoftaj
YouTube: https://www.youtube.com/@sailingcatalpa
Facebook: https://www.facebook.com/sailingcatalpa/
Website: https://www.sailingcatalpa.com

Tranquillity
Instagram: @bkroon75
YouTube: https://www.youtube.com/@SVTranquillity

Carina of Devon
Website: https://carinaofdevon.wordpress.com

Health and safety
Pediatric and bespoke medical kits: https://www.msos.org.uk/

Homemade sunscreen recipe: https://iquitplastics.com/blog/reef-safe-sunscreen-recipe?format=amp

Infant formula preparation guidelines: https://www.cdc.gov/nutrition/infantandtoddlernutrition/formula-feeding/infant-formula-preparation-and-storage.html

World Health Organization childhood immunization guidelines: https://www.who.int/teams/immunization-vaccines-and-biologicals/policies/who-recommendations-for-routine-immunization---summary-tables

Safety swimming courses: https://infantaquatics.com/

Keith Colwell, *Sea Survival Handbook*, RYA

Learn to sail
Find a certified sailing or weather course:
Vagabonde Adventures (our own certification and charter company): https://www.vagabondeadventures.com
American Sailing Association: https://asa.com
Royal Yachting Association: https://www.rya.org.uk/training/sail-cruising

Guides to sailing:
Vagabonde Essential Sail Guide: https://sailinglavagabonde.shop/products/the-slv-essential-sail-guide

Hal Roth, *How to sail around the world*. Roth.

Jimmy Cornell, *World cruising routes*. Adlard Coles Nautical.

Education

Yachting World Top Tips: https://www.yachtingworld.com/practical-cruising/home-schooling-at-sea-top-tips-tutoring-kids-liveaboard-sailors-126507

Online learning:

Khan Academy: https://www.khanacademy.org
ABC Mouse: https://www.abcmouse.com
BBC Bite Size: https://www.bbc.co.uk/bitesize
IXL Maths and English practice: https://uk.ixl.com/

Sea specific citizen science projects:

https://www.oceanoculus.com/news-from-the-sea/community-citizen-science-project
https://oceanservice.noaa.gov/citizen-science/
https://goesfoundation.com/
https://www.seakeepers.org/citizen-science/

Unschooling:

John Holt, *Learning all the time*, DaCapo Lifelong Books.
Clark Aldrich, *Unschooling rules*, Greenleaf Book Group.

Acknowledgements

First and foremost, to my boys, Lenny and Darwin, you've been my greatest adventure, my best teachers, and my reason to keep going when the seas (and the schoolwork) got rough. To my partner, Riley, for holding the helm with me through every storm, for sharing this crazy dream from the very start, and for entertaining the children while I wrote this book.

To the incredible community of travelling families, including sailors, caravaners, vanlifers and wanderers, who have shared anchorages, campfires, advice and friendship along the way. You have reminded me that deep down, most people are kind and eager to help, and that there is always someone ready to lend a hand or share a laugh.

A huge thank you to Martina Tyrrell, writer, editor and kindred spirit, for helping me gather the voices of so many inspiring families and for turning my scrappy journal-style ramblings into something approachable, clear and, I hope, enjoyable for all.

To the creators, bloggers and YouTubers who generously share their hard-earned wisdom, making the journey a little easier for those who follow.

And finally, to every child growing up on the move, this book is for you. May you always carry your sense of wonder, no matter where the tide or the road takes you.

– Elayna

www.ingramcontent.com/pod-product-compliance
Lightning Source LLC
Chambersburg PA
CBHW021226090426
42740CB00006B/404